LIFE PASSAGES FOR MEN

Life Passages for Men

Understanding the Stages in a Man's Life

E. James Wilder

Servant Publications
Ann Arbor, Michigan

Vine Books is an imprint of Servant Publications
especially designed to serve Evangelical Christians.

Published by Servant Publications
P.O. Box 8617
Ann Arbor, Michigan 48107

The names and characterizations in this book drawn from the
author's personal experience are rendered pseudonymously and
many times as fictional composites. Any similarity between the
names and characterizations of these individuals and real people
is unintended and purely coincidental.

Cover design by Steve Eames

93 94 95 96 97 10 9 8 7 6 5 4 3 2 1

Printed in the United States of America
ISBN 0-89283-835-3

Library of Congress Cataloging-in-Publication Data

Wilder, E. James, 1952–
    Life passages for men : understanding the stages in a man's life /
E. James Wilder.
    222 p.   cm.
    Includes bibliographical references.
    ISBN 0-89283-835-3
    1. Men (Christian theology) I. Title.
BT703.5.W544   1993
248.8'42—dc20   93-6056

Contents

Acknowledgments / 7
Preface / 9
Introduction / 11

1. Becoming a Boy / 19
2. A Boy and His Mother / 33
3. A Boy and His Father / 51
4. The Man Who Has Never Been a Boy / 65
5. Becoming a Man / 75
6. Three Killer Myths / 87
7. How Sons Become Men / 97
8. Life-Giving Manly Roles / 107
9. Becoming a Father / 121
10. Fathers and Their Children / 131
11. The Father's World / 151
12. Single and Childless Men as Fathers / 165
13. Becoming an Elder / 173
14. The Elder and His Sons / 187
15. The Elder and His Daughters / 195
16. Elders and the Church / 205
17. The Death of an Elder / 213

Notes / 221

ACKNOWLEDGMENTS

DAVE CAME OF SERVANT PUBLICATIONS was instrumental in the inception and completion of this book. Without his eagerness this would still be one of those books I should write some day. Dave was a clear, direct negotiator and practiced in his work the spirit of Christian manhood.

My good friends Rick Koepcke and Gary Bayer supported me through some of the hardest growing up I ever hope to do. They have helped me be a father. Merv Dirks has shown me much of what I know of being an elder; he is an inspiration and a man of God.

Michael A. Jones allowed me the use of the computers and facilities at Christensen & Jones for the editing and completion of this book. He is my wife's employer and takes an interest in our children and community. The way he handles his business, which is retirement accounts, shows his concern for the future well-being of others. Mike is a playful boss. He demonstrates in his life a blend of boy, man, father, and elder which set him apart as an example to emulate.

WHEN IT COMES TIME FOR EVERY BOY to become a man, he waits in desperate need of a treasure, the essence of which each man possesses and every boy desires. Each boy—whether he knows it or not—waits for the elders of his tribe, clan, family, neighborhood, or church to fill in that missing part of what it means to be a man. This book contains the first account of this secret treasure for the boys and men of this generation.

The essence of manhood is not our sensitivity. It is not the wild man within. It is not our call to commitment. It is not even the offer of healing that may help to make men out of wounded boys. All these things may play their part in helping us become men, but the essence is the supreme gift of receiving and then understanding our own history as a man. Without this knowledge, neither men nor women will be able to recognize and appreciate masculinity in their fathers, sons, brothers, husbands, or male friends. Opening this treasure entails knowing how a man develops and then passes through the stages of his life.

To the younger men I say, "Come with me, my son, as I tell you the secret of the elders, as they themselves have shown it to me. Let us go apart and you will come to know in time the history of your people—your kind. My son, your history is your heritage. It is your destiny. Its words are written in your soul.

"A word of instruction to you, my son: You will need to read this book to the end before you understand the beginning. Without the beginning, you cannot know the end. Without beginning or end, you cannot even see your face or find your feet.

"Remember, my son, that the secret of men and their history is not something you must ever try to hide. You and I need not hide it from women, children, or even from men who appear to be less than what they were meant to be. This is one of God's secrets which could be exposed in broad daylight, right in front of you, and still you would not be able to see it. You will only see it clearly and understand it with some measure of fullness when your time has come and the elders have taught you to see. You may live this secret boldly and talk of it before others. As you do, people will be amazed at you and wonder what it is that makes you a man."

To the younger women I say, "My daughter, come with me and I will teach you the secret of what makes a man. You, too, should know how to recognize and read the soul of a man. Otherwise, boys will be the bane of your life and pretenders will plague your heart. If you do not learn this secret, we will be strangers, you and I; your brother will be a loss; your husband, a foe; and your son, an enigma, or even a threat.

"You must know that a man cannot be tamed, even if you start trying when he is but a baby. Neither your love nor your anger can make him a man, for his life as a man comes from his elders, not from you. Strange as this truth may sound to you, it has always been known.

"A word of instruction to you, my daughter: stay close to me until the end and you will understand the beginning, if this is your time. You must know that no one can teach a secret when it is not the time."

To the older men and women I say: "It is your special privilege to insure that these secrets become known by the young people around you. Many people do not even know that they need this knowledge. They will learn only if you take time to appreciate them and their young ways. I hope you will add your own words to those of this book."

INTRODUCTION

MOST OF THE MEN I KNOW have real trouble saying when exactly each of them became a man. Many of us men still feel like little boys inside. We are not sure exactly what it means to be a man. Yet every man goes through a life cycle that seems both familiar and alien. We are born babies and grow into boys, then men, often becoming fathers and finally grandfathers or elders. This process was easier to understand when the world didn't move so fast, but it seems that today we need to review how it works. That's what this book is about. When we are done, I hope you will say, "I knew that, but I never thought of it that way before."

It works like this: each phase of life has a main task to master and each stage builds on the previous one, just as the primer and finish coats are added, one step at a time, when you are painting a house. Growing up male is a four-step process. If we get the steps in the right order and do a reasonably good job at them, we will be satisfied with the results. Otherwise, like a bad paint job on a house, we will be cracking, blistering, and peeling every time things get hot.

Why is it that men aren't more in touch with themselves? A few years ago a book came out on the subject of men who hated women. I bought a copy at a large bookstore, and as I paid for it the clerk commented that in the year since the book had come out, I was the first man with the courage to buy a copy. This is a sad commentary on the self-awareness of men who without mirrors for their souls can't even reflect that something is wrong inside. Yet I am convinced that man hating is also a problem. Many men I have met even hate themselves! People in the recovery movement often voice doubts to me about men because of the abuse they have suffered.

Sometimes people hear every positive statement about men as a denial of the damage men can do, or as a negative statement about women. This is not my intent. When I say that to be a man is good, I don't mean as compared to being a woman. Instead it is a reminder that when God looked at his creation, he said that it was good just as it stood.

In a sense, this book is simple, but simple is not necessarily easy. Being a man is a good thing. To reach maturity every man must go through four life stages and complete four essential tasks. Each stage builds on the one before rather than replacing it. However, it is hard work successfully negotiating the passage from one stage to the next and living authentically.

The principles that govern life are quite simple as well. It often helps us to look at these principles one at a time in order to learn how they work. If we take a few of these simple principles and look at them clearly, it helps us make sense of life a bit better. A firm grasp of simple principles helps us understand complex processes without needing to memorize every detail. For instance, knowing how to multiply lets me figure out the answer to 2789.3 multiplied by 10 without needing to memorize my 2789.3 tables. Understanding principles helps us think through issues on our own. So when we learn principles we can reach the same conclusions and solutions each time, even if we forget the details.

Let me give you an example. I asked a friend of mine how he decided which way to vote on complex ballot propositions. He answered that since he was against big government, he voted for everything that made government smaller and against anything that made it bigger. He voted against anything that increased debt and for everything that decreased debt. With these two principles in mind, he rarely had trouble making a choice on election day.

If the principles that we select are sound, then we can clarify our choices and decisions in helpful ways. In fact, all of this book can be seen as an expansion of one simple principle that I believe is found clearly in Scripture: God and the people he made like himself are a meaningful part of history. Or put another way, God has a purpose in history. The whole Bible and the account of God's action in the church can be viewed as a history lesson. It is in history that we meet God and he meets us.

History tells us what has happened and what it means. Each of us has a history, but ours is not complete until we know what it means. If we don't understand what has happened to us, we cannot understand our history and will not know who we really are.

There are several ways of finding a meaning in history. There are different perspectives to take when viewing the same events. But the perspective that we all need to gain is what I call "the eyes of heaven." We cannot see the true meaning of what has happened to us until we have seen it clearly from God's perspective.

For example, here is a bit of history that changed when seen through the eyes of heaven. One Friday there is a crucifixion of an innocent man. On the following Sunday two of his friends are walking along a road with a stranger who has heard of the crucifixion but seems to have no appreciation for the meaning that it had for these two grieving friends. These men are shocked that this mysterious stranger does not seem to appreciate the tragic turn that history has just taken. They ask him in effect, "Don't you know what has happened here in the last few days?"

As the stranger begins to talk to them about the same history that they have just concluded is the worst tragedy in the history of Jerusalem, he lets them know that if they look through the eyes of heaven they will see something marvelous has just transpired. So by the time the trio reaches Emmaus, the destination of the two friends, they have a much different view of what has just occurred.

Had the facts changed in any way during the walk? Not really, but the friends now had the view from heaven that gave new meaning to what they knew. All of us have moments in our history that constitute major problems, hurts, confusion, and even evil events. When we look at our world, it has the same sorts of problems in it. We can look at it from different perspectives, but until we have the eyes of heaven we won't know the meaning of the events. We won't know who we are in our own history until we begin to realize its significance. That is usually the hard part.

Here, then, is the history of a man in four easy steps or four parts. These are the four stages that we either go through, or end up wishing we had. Each stage builds on the one before:

> *The Boy*—knows his needs and feelings
> *The Man*—becomes a part of history
> *The Father*—gives life to others
> *The Grandfather*—reaches beyond his own house

If you work diligently at each of these steps and keep them in the right order, you will be blessed and admired as a mature, fulfilled, and fruitful man. You will be a reminder to everyone that to be a man is really a good thing. Yes, indeed, being a man is a good thing just as being a woman is a good thing.

UNDERSTANDING OUR LEVEL OF NEED

Now that we have reviewed the basic building blocks of a man's history, we can turn our attention to the fascinating details of growing up male. The intricacy of each male reveals the beauty of who he is meant to be. To see such a sight, we must approach quite close and become quite personal. Men who don't know that they need intimacy will find this very uncomfortable or even repulsive. Yet, in order to understand the boy, we must overcome our anxiety and draw quite close to the boy, his body and his needs.

Intimacy is a word that often carries sexual connotations, but it can also mean something close and personal, inside the limits of our defenses. One way of understanding and measuring intimacy is to see how people handle their needs. It is not desirable to be needy in our culture, so revealing needs is something that most people, particularly men, are hesitant to do. This makes sharing one's needs a good indicator of intimacy.

There are four levels of sharing needs:

1. I once had a need.
2. I just had a need.
3. I have a specific need.
4. I need something, but I don't know what it is.

I once had a need. This is like some of the old-time revival meetings where a repentant sinner would testify that as a youngster he did bad things and needed help, but that was years ago. Now, thank God, he is free of such problems. This type of sharing is the first step into intimacy, for it reveals to us a history we might not otherwise have known.

I just had a need. This sort of a need is commonly expressed in sharing or support groups. Last week I felt really depressed, or I had no money. But, thank God, he answered my prayers, and today I am much better and ready to thank him. People often get stuck on this level because they are afraid to make themselves vulnerable. But there may be good reasons to preclude any deeper intimacy—at least, for a time.

I have a specific need. This is the third level of intimacy and gives most people a sense of being exposed and vulnerable. This can be very hard to do, especially for men. At this level, someone might say, "I am lonely," or "I need new tires and I can't afford them," directly to others. This is the deepest level of intimacy that many people ever achieve as adults.

I need something, but I don't know what it is. This is the deepest level of intimacy. At this level, people know that something is wrong, but for the life of them they can't figure out what it is. Such people are easily exploited by others. This is the level that advertising tries to reach by showing us intimate things that we don't talk about, and then telling us that what we need is their product. It is at this level that each baby boy begins his struggle to learn what it means to be a boy.

This need continues throughout life. We all need people who can tell us who we are when we can't figure it out, people who see us through the eyes of God. Little boys start out completely helpless in this way. They do not know who they are or what they need.

Take for example a little boy who won't go to sleep. He wanders out into the living room, fussing. When his mom or dad or the babysitter sees him, he hears, "You stupid, spoiled little brat, go to bed!" (Now he knows who he is according to the ones who speak for God.) "You need a good spanking!" (Now he knows what he needs.) From that point on the little boy knows who he is and what he needs. It becomes a part of his identity. Whenever he feels upset in later life, he may remember this object lesson which defined him. So the next time he feels upset he knows how to act and what to look for. He will look for someone to yell at him and tell him something like, "You stupid, spoiled little brat," and then spank him. He might have to provoke his wife or girlfriend for quite some time before she meets his needs, but then he will settle down. At the same time he and his mate might begin to ask each other, "Why do we have to go through this each time?" or, "Why does it always end this way?"

The question we need to ask is, who did God see when that little boy walked into the living room? Is that who God would have said was there and what that boy needed? I don't think so, yet all of us start becoming boys with the need to be told who we are. The people that raise us have the first and greatest chance to determine our identity. If they do a good job of it, we can count ourselves blessed. But even if they don't, God has the last say because if the identity they give us is trash, it won't withstand the heat of life and soon will begin to crumble into ashes.

Then, like the two disciples on the road to Emmaus, we may be ready for our own resurrection experience, which helps us make sense of the pain in our lives.

ONE

Becoming a Boy

BIRTH—THE FIRST PASSAGE

"IT'S A BOY!" What a good thing has happened—a boy has been born and that is just what God wanted this time. That makes him very valuable. After such a good start will he become the man that God intended him to become? New fathers and mothers have been known to feel overwhelmed at the potential and the needs latent in each child.

"It's a boy!" Tomorrow we will want to know how many ounces he has lost, and the day after that how many he has gained. The measuring of his progress is well under way. He is completely a boy and yet so much less than a boy must become.

"It's a boy!" He is a product of the history that went before him. That history will even determine his name. And he is an enigma right now because his very birth has started history in a different direction than before his birth and no one knows where it will lead.

"It's a boy!" That means blue clothes. He will probably shop in auto parts stores and attend lots of sports events. On the average, he will receive far fewer offers to hold a baby or sew a dress and may never choose to use mascara. We have ideas as a culture that will shape his growth.

The boy has joined the stream of life. A stream both too wide and too deep for him to comprehend. And yet, life is really simple. Rivers are made of drops of water. Drops are made of molecules. It is just that there are quite a few simple things in life, and when you combine that many simple things it becomes a bit overwhelming at first. To gain a general understanding of life a boy must learn to reach even beyond old age. So we will outline the four stages and six passages every male must face. His success is not guaranteed and the difficulty level is high. If he succeeds it will cost him his life, if he fails he will lose his life.

Becoming a boy: the first stage. Now that birth, his first passage, is completed, the boy is alive. Becoming a boy is his first job after he is born. It is not an easy job and will take the first twelve years of his life. All the same it is a simple job to be a boy. The boy's task is to learn to receive what he needs and express what he feels. That is the task of childhood.

Every boy must work his way along this difficult process, learning as he goes what he needs and who he is. Even Jesus started out as a boy. It seems to bother some Christmas story-tellers that all the Gospels have recorded about Jesus as a child is that he received from others. He works no miracles for little drummer boys, no healings for his parents, no dividing his lunch among five thousand people. In spite of the traditional carol's statement that while in the manger the little Lord Jesus did not cry, there is no scriptural support for that view. Every indication supports the idea that he expressed his needs and feelings and received from others what he did not earn. Jesus was a boy on the road to becoming a man.

Fundamentally, it isn't any different for little girls. They must pass through the same sorts of stages and passages with some subtle differences, but this is a book about boys and men. Boys and men need to know that the foundation for life is to receive what you have not earned without shame. This is part of why to enter the kingdom of God one must become like a little child— in our case, a boy. We express our needs and receive without condemnation or shame. Boys are not born knowing what they want or feel, so this becomes the first stage of growth. This is the art of being a boy; you express your need and receive in return. By the time boyhood is over at age twelve, every boy should have mastered expressing his needs and feelings and receiving what he asks for without shame.

Curiously, many of the experts on child development have been men. Jean Piaget developed his stages and theories by observing his own children. Due to their hair-raising complexity, his theories are usually left to intellectuals. The developmental theorist Erick Erikson advocated a far more digestible model of human development which he divided into eight stages, each one with its own crisis. Later writers, such as Horval Hendricks, have developed descriptions of what adults are like if they get stuck at one of these developmental crises. Hendricks particularly focuses on the effects which getting stuck produces in love relationships and mate selection. Notice the importance of this connection between the failure to grow up properly and adult life. Omitting or distorting any stage of development will produce a deficit in all the stages that come afterwards. We must not only choose the foundation carefully but watch what we build upon it.

I mention Erikson's eight crises here with some description of each one, so they can provide us with a baseline of comparison for my own stages and passages, especially in my next two chapters about the importance of a boy's relationship with his mother and then his father early in his development. In my later chapters about fathers and elders, I find Erikson's analysis less helpful.

1. Basic Trust Versus Basic Mistrust: ages 0-1, I am what I am given. The boy's identity develops out of what he is given and how he is treated.

2. Autonomy Versus Shame and Doubt: ages 1-3, I am what I will. The child thinks of himself in terms of what he can do often, pulling his hand away and insisting on doing things himself.

3. Initiative Versus Guilt: ages 3-6, I am what I imagine I will be. The boy becomes the things and people he dreams he is. He loves to pretend and try new things.

4. Industry Versus Inferiority: ages 6-13, I am what I learn. The child begins to see that he must learn things he does not yet know. He sets out on quests, adventures, and conquests. Dreams become real.

5. Identity Versus Identity Diffusion: ages 13-19, I am all of the above. Each aspect of identity must be combined with the others to become a man who contains all these attributes.

6. Intimacy Versus Isolation: Young adult. He must now learn to maintain himself in close harmony with others.

7. Productivity Versus Self-Absorption: Adulthood. He is now challenged to be the source of good things.

8. Integrity Versus Despair: Maturity. Now his soul must be capable of maintaining itself and his influence even if he loses some abilities or strength.

Perhaps it will take the full trip through a man's life to understand the importance that the first stages and passages have for the last ones and how hazardous the trip becomes without the gifts of the very old to guide the very young. What may at first seem overwhelmingly complex becomes a single, deep, and complex rhythm of variations on the same theme—how to receive and then give life.

The unweaned infant boy. In chapter two we will look extensively at the unweaned boy and the four years of preparation he needs to complete Erikson's first two crises in time for weaning. By weaning, I mean not simply being weaned from the breast or even a bottle but a whole set of behaviors and attitudes whereby the boy separates from his mother and achieves a basic level of independence, usually around age four. *(This broader under - standing of weaning is very important to keep in mind throughout this book.)* However, in our culture, weaning is rarely timed to coincide with when the child will no longer be breast-fed or even bottle-fed. We rush our children into independence as fast as possible.

WEANING—THE SECOND PASSAGE

Weaning is the boy's introduction to his father's world once he is old enough to take basic care of himself and separate from his mother. This major passage occurs right in the middle of childhood. It begins to usher him into the world outside his home and prepares him to negotiate the later passage into manhood. We will explore the world of the weaned boy in some depth in chapter three. Here are three general considerations about a boy's childhood after weaning.

1. The boy develops an identity. Boys practice their identity as they go along. Much of this practice is what we call play. It is play because the outcome is not so serious. In play, boys try out their ideas of how to participate in life. A boy with a poorly built identity can sometimes get by while he is playing only to collapse under real-life strain. But one with a proper identity will build strength and variety during play. Boys need to play.

Just as each phase of development builds on the previous one without removing it, there are ways in which development can be anticipated. Play often includes elements of preparation for future tasks. Kittens play in mock fights preparing for territorial disputes later on in life. They practice pouncing and stalking each other in preparation for hunting. Kittens lick each other in preparation for becoming mothers. Little boys also prepare to become men in their play. They may watch super heroes on TV in order to be a hero like Dad when they grow up. In some parts of the world they shoot at melons with their bows and arrows to hone their hunting skills.

The best arena for practicing being a father is in being a brother and a friend to others. That prepares a boy to be a man. Since it is play time, the roles are not clearly defined. That is to say, a brother can practice being both a man and a father with his siblings as can a friend with his friends, but there is a difference.

You cannot spend much time around little boys without discovering that "fairness" is a big deal. While some writers think it is a bad thing that boys typically spend just as much time arguing about the rules as playing the game, I believe that both are essential to play. Arguing is playing at the man's role of making things fair for all sides. People who want to make little boys into little girls dislike this kind of play because it doesn't advance the harmonious play of the game. If we judge by how much fairness boys achieve in a particular contest, then we might agree with the critics. In actuality, this type of play usually comes as far from producing fairness as shooting little play arrows into green melons is from hunting wild boar. But play is play. It should not be measured by the same yardstick adults use.

Without the active intervention of adults to help a boy achieve an adult sense of fairness and history, he may turn fairness issues into control fights over rules as he grows older. But boys have their friends and siblings to practice on to learn what fairness is.

One way we helped our two sons Jamie and Rami (Rami rhymes with Jamie) prepare for fairness was to make it a family rule that they must work out conflicts between themselves. Even though Jamie was four at the time and Rami was two, working things out was their job. We informed them of the simple ground rules. If they brought a dispute to our attention or requested an intervention, they were told to sit at a table, and neither one could get up until the other one gave him permission. Sometimes negotiations were very loud and other times silent. The longest session was close to two hours, as I recall. Did they achieve fairness? I never checked so I don't know, they were just preparing. It did not take long for them, however, to realize the value of mutually acceptable solutions. On one occasion they were simply not able to solve the problem without adult help and both agreed to find that help together. Adult intervention is key at times when real fairness is needed. We will talk more about teaching fairness when we discuss becoming men.

Brothers are asked at times to go beyond fairness and care for their brothers and sisters because the need is there, even if it is not fair at the moment. In this way being a brother can also prepare a boy to be a father. Provided that the practice is not too intensive and draining, most boys will find it gratifying. As with piano lessons, too much of a good thing will kill anyone's interest. Lack of encouragement will also destroy a boy's interest in difficult tasks. In addition, there is quite a range of responses among boys. Some respond well, others say they will never play the piano or take care of anyone again. Opportunities do not guarantee success.

2. A boy learns satisfaction. By the time he reaches twelve years of age, every boy should be very fluent in saying what he feels and knowing what he needs. He should be able to take in everything that the world has to offer that is good and reject the bad. The boy should know how to be satisfied.

Finding satisfaction is a very important job. Without it a boy will not be able to meet his needs. It takes a while to learn how to do this well. The road to learning what meets a boy's needs is long and difficult at times. Incredible as it seems toddlers will drink gasoline, drain cleaner, and many other things that older children will spit out instantly, recognizing that gasoline will not quench their thirst.

While finding out what he should drink is part of what a young child must learn, each year the problems become more complex. One sunny afternoon my sons discovered some facts about satisfaction. The lesson came from a ladder they found in the garage. With this new toy, they could climb on the garage roof and see all around. One time Rami was on the roof and instructed his older brother Jamie who was still on the ground to help him get down. Jamie simply pushed the ladder away from the roof, giving Rami a quick ride to the ground. Rami's feelings told Jamie instantly that was not the way to meet his needs in the future. Fast and impulsive results were not the most satisfying.

As a twelve-year-old, one of my sons faced a teacher who was very unfair and controlling. This made my son quite angry on a regular basis. Expressing his anger directly to the teacher was not allowed, so he decided to get back at the teacher by not doing any of his homework. Not doing homework drove his teacher wild, and she would explode each time the assignments were missing. This solution helped him express his anger indirectly but did not meet his need to learn. Unlike declining gasoline in favor of water, this conflict of needs and feelings proved harder to untangle.

By the time a boy reaches twelve, he should have learned how to be satisfied, and that dissatisfaction is not so bad because it is temporary. The satisfied boy knows how to meet his needs and can choose well between competing solutions.

Tragically, the majority of men do not appear to have finished the job of being a boy. Most of them do not know what they feel or how to meet their needs. This leaves them very vulnerable. When we are dissatisfied and do not know what satisfies us, we are sitting ducks for anyone who claims to have an answer.

Advertising, for example, is the fine art of creating dissatisfaction. The main purpose of most modern advertising is to create a feeling of dissatisfaction and then tell us what will meet that need. If boys and men knew what they felt and what met their needs, such seductive advertising would have no impact. The sales of brand-name beer, tires, and luxury cars—to name a few—would plummet and put advertising agencies out of business.

If we know what we need, there is no use for advertising except to tell us where something we may really need is available. The popularity of advertising and the way most men succumb to it tells me that men have not finished being boys and do not know what they feel or need. Many men simply have not taken care of that first twelve-year job.

3. A boy learns about grace. Just as each stage of life has its job, each job has its purpose. The purpose of the first stage of development is to learn about grace. This is how we learn about our intrinsic value. The twelve years of boyhood are the time to learn how to receive grace. Grace is gifts given freely. We do not earn these or perform for them. These gifts are given because someone has decided that we are worth it, just because they think so.

All of us have value, because we were created in God's image. We have value because God has said that we have value. It is not because of anything we have done. As boys we should all have the opportunity to learn this lesson so that without any doubt in our mind we should, by the time we are twelve, know we have great value without having to do anything at all.

A moment of self-examination will cause most people to discover that they feel their value comes from what they can do. If they couldn't earn a living, talk and think straight, if they couldn't contribute to their family or society, they would think that they had lost much of their value. Boys who never learn how to receive grace become men who turn to achievements, fame, and fortune in order to find value. They must *do* something to feel valuable and so they don't really know who they are.

Our culture is not going to tell us who we really are. God tells us we have great value for just being made in his image, so it is only if we look at ourselves from his point of view that we realize we have great value, even if we can't do anything at all.

The need to receive is with us all of our lives. Being boys simply is our time to learn what really satisfies. We will need this skill in every later stage of our lives. Each of these stages builds on the previous stage. This makes life increasingly complex.

I just taught my younger son Rami to drive. First we worked on the accelerator, then the clutch and the brake. At first, he would forget what he had learned about the accelerator when he used the clutch. Then we added steering, and he almost forgot the clutch, but he sure hit the brakes hard. In time, we added driving in traffic to the tasks and thankfully he remembered the previous steps. So it is with growing up, each stage builds on the previous ones. As soon as we start thinking that we no longer need to keep in mind what we learned in a previous stage, we will hit major snags in our growth.

THE THIRD PASSAGE BRINGS THE SECOND STAGE— BECOMING A MAN

We become men at around age thirteen. The new job for this stage is also very simple. A man makes things fair for himself and others. Rather than just receive and think about his own needs and feelings, a man thinks equally about his needs or feelings and those of others.

The job of being a man teaches him to drive a hard bargain, to reach what is fair for him and what is fair for another. A man doesn't just take care of his own needs or look out for himself, he looks out for the other person's needs as though they were as important as his own. When a man does business, the person he is dealing with gets equal, fair treatment.

It takes a while to go from being totally self-centered as a boy to becoming a man. This stage of development usually takes one up to the early twenties, say twenty-one, to pick an arbitrary number. By that time, a man should be able to bargain hard, get a fair deal, not be intimidated by other men, and get fair exchange and fair value.

The purpose of manhood is to help boys become a part of history. By joining the stream of history, a man comes to know that what he does has an impact on other people. Therefore he must be careful about what he does to insure that his impact on history (or his story) is a good one. A good man wants his effect to be good, fair, peaceful, and just. That is what becoming a man is about. Everything he does influences history, so care is necessary to insure that it will be pleasing when seen through the eyes of heaven. By the time a man gets to be about twenty-one, he should have that job whipped, though perhaps most of us don't.

THE FOURTH PASSAGE BRINGS THE THIRD STAGE—BECOMING A FATHER

To become a father, a man adds the job of unselfish giving to that of knowing what he needs and feels as well as looking out for others like he does for himself. As a father, he learns to give without getting in return. That is the main job of being a father.

You know that you are a father when your child has kept you up all night, screaming in your ear, spitting up on you, and showing no appreciation at all for your efforts. When the man goes to work the next day, tired and crabby, he might warn others to keep out of his way because "his kid kept him up all night," but inside he knows he is a father. He has given unselfishly. He knows that he needed and deserved sleep and could have insisted that his child allow him to meet his needs. Or he could have bargained hard and been a man, "I'll stay up with you tonight, but tomorrow night you stay up and carry me around." Of course, he didn't. Instead, the father gave without getting in return and knows he is a dad. Now his child is learning the same lesson about having value without having to do anything to deserve it.

The father passes on the gift of grace he received by his unselfish giving. By staying up all night, he says, "You, my child, have great value to me even if you keep me up all night, spit up all over me, mess in your diapers, and scream and yell in my ear. Even if you do not care that I am here, you have enough value to lose sleep over." That is a dad's heart.

He knows what he needs. No one stays up all night and says, "I never need to sleep." He can express his feelings about it as well, "I'm tired, but I love my child." He can go to work and drive a hard bargain, but at home he is free to move beyond into unselfish giving. Only the man who has completed the first two stages can give freely and wisely.

The purpose of fatherhood is to imitate God the Father in our family. The chance to stand in for God is the greatest honor that anyone can have. The father becomes an example of who God is to his family. That is the purpose for unselfish giving by the father. This task also takes a while to learn. It is as simple and difficult as both of the previous steps and takes about as long to learn. A father is getting the hang of it about the time his children become teens. By that time, unselfishness should be second nature to good old Dad.

THE FIFTH PASSAGE BRINGS THE FOURTH STAGE— BECOMING AN ELDER

Now that his children have become men and women, a man is ready to learn the fourth and final step of his development, becoming an elder or grandfather. A truly *Grand Father* is one who is able to treat children who are not biologically his own with the same unselfish giving he learned to give to his own. An elder is a father to his community. He is a father to those who were not fortunate enough to have a father who imitated God's unselfish giving or who lost their fathers due to premature death or other catastrophic losses.

There are many people who have not been raised under the care of the good kind of father I have just described, so there is no shortage of people who could use an elder or a grandfather. One problem with our society is that we often expect older people to buy a Winnebago and drive off into the sunset. There is no concept that we are to adopt the fatherless at that point. We, therefore, have few elders, few spare fathers, few people willing to care for those in real need. There is a great lack in our churches and communities of elders. There are many men who have grown into their sixties still waiting to meet someone who is a father capable of telling them, "You are now a man."

The purpose of the elder stage. The decline of fathers and elders in our culture has produced an ever increasing interest in God as our Father. Fortunately, God has promised to be a father to the fatherless, but that does not mean that he intends for the rest of us to avoid that role. On the contrary, he desperately needs men who can walk in his grace and fulfill that role for the fatherless, who are his children. If I had my way about it, I'd have each of you sit down with an elder and learn to see yourself through the eyes of heaven.

THE FINAL PASSAGE—DEATH

Having prepared for five other passages and having endured the first completely unprepared but surrounded by loving support, every man must face his greatest transformation into a stage beyond our view. When elders die, it is a time of great blessing and not to be missed.

The purpose of death. Death is the final decontamination process from all that may have gone wrong in our lives. All that is life-receiving and life-giving lives on, everything that is death-dealing finally dies. That is why witnessing the death of an elder is such a blessed experience.

CONCLUSION

There is no way to talk about a boy and his needs or feelings without discussing his relationship to the two most important figures in his life, his mother and father. The impact of these figures or their absence has telling effects on how a boy will learn to do his job. The next two chapters will discuss a boy and his mother and a boy and his father, whether the boy's parents were physically present to him or not.

Yes, a boy is a wonder, a treasure of great value, as is every girl. How we are honored when one is placed in our care. May we have eyes to see treasures in each little boy, even the one we once were.

TWO

A Boy and His Mother

But Mary treasured all these things and pondered them in her heart. Luke 2:19

O UR SECOND SON WAS BORN at home on the kitchen table. Before the cord was cut, he had cried and started nursing at his mother's breast. His mother had wanted him to be born at home surrounded by family. Linda, our neighbor, was waiting downstairs to hear the news and started the phone calls as soon as the shout reached her through the back window, "It's a boy, Linda!" My wife just smiled and reached for the baby.

We had been to many classes and doctor's visits to prepare for childbirth at home. We had watched movies and read books. We had talked to doctors, nurses, midwives, mothers who had chosen home-births, and people from Third World countries where children were usually born at home. Unlike all the preparation we needed for giving birth, our boy started on his main work immediately. Within the first two minutes of birth, he cried to express his need and then received from his mother's supply of milk. Our baby was becoming a boy.

MOTHER AND THE UNWEANED SON

Strange that the first thing our boy needed was to nurse at a breast. Does it seem uncomfortable to think and talk about needs that way? To understand what it takes to be a boy, we need to look intimately at the boy's needs from his perspective. Meeting these needs is his first order of business for the next twelve years. A boy needs a breast or a baby bottle. It will keep him alive, content, comforted, busy, and connected to his world. To him it is love, acceptance, food, life, activity, warmth, something to see and touch, and something to make him feel better. The breast then becomes a metaphor for the life-giving bond between son and mother. Although the sensual, emotional, and nutritional value of breastfeeding cannot be matched, it is the nature of the bond between son and mother that is of crucial concern, not whether the boy gets his nutrients and calories from his mother's breast or a baby bottle. For about the next four years, she will be largely responsible for the quality of his life until he is weaned and ready to care for himself.

Take a few moments to imagine a baby boy's world. The baby's new world is a very unfamiliar place of sudden changes and a few constants. In the midst of confusion there are the regular and relaxing workouts on Mother's breast or his baby bottle. To him it almost always is simply warm life and satisfaction. The boy needs his connection to the breast. This connection brings life. From this connection, he begins to understand all other connections in his life. This is how the basic trust mentioned by Erikson in his first crisis begins to grow, for without this core the boy will mistrust the world, people, and himself.

The boy asks and receives. He neither knows at first that he is asking or receiving. Mother knows his cry is asking. She knows the way he turns his head towards her is asking. She knows that his tugging at her blouse is asking, so she teaches him by saying, "Is my little boy hungry?" He learns that he needs something and he learns to ask. He did not know that before.

It is with Mother's help that the boy will learn that he has needs. Mother guesses these needs from his cries and actions. She guesses he is too hot or too cold, that he needs a nap or needs to be burped. Perhaps she guesses his cry means a new tooth is coming in, and he needs something to chew. Mother recognizes and intuitively knows that his cries ask for something. From within her come the words to fulfill his request. Slowly and in time the boy learns to use words to express his needs until one day they are expected from him. When that day comes, Mother will say, "How do you ask?" which means he forgot to say, "Please."

It is not my intention in writing about mothers to tell mothers how to be mothers. In fact, it seems that mothers are the only ones qualified to have the final say about what is maternal and what isn't. I am explaining to men what a mother is like in relation to her baby boy so that men can put into words what it is that a mother does. As an observer, I can describe what I see mothers doing. What follows is, therefore, descriptive not normative.

Mother is the first source of connection for a boy. From his connection with Mommy he learns many things: he learns to eat, to sleep, to take in what is good, and to cry for what he wants. With Mother's help and guesses, the boy learns how to find all the essential things he will ever really need. He also learns about his own body—where it starts and ends, its powers and limitations.

The mother of a dependent, unweaned child is truly a marvel of creation. This mother knows not only when he is sleepy, hungry, and wet, but when he needs attention and is curious. Further, she thinks he is marvelous and lets him know that. This mother even likes to share the joy of having him with others. She knows that he needs more love than just her own and fills his life with good people while he still does not know he needs them.

Perhaps the main person that Mother shares him with is his dad, but older siblings are very important as well. The good mother finds other mothers for her child, so that he may benefit from more care and attention than she can provide. Love is not threatened by such sharing. Often these other mothers are female relatives, sometimes they are close friends. Together they explore and enjoy the uniqueness of her son. He, in turn, learns that love is to be shared, not hoarded.

Pity the poor boy whose mother does not sense his needs or respond well to them. She feeds him when she is hungry, or sends him to play when she wants to watch television, and holds him when she needs reassurance. He approaches weaning with a desperate need to be connected because he hasn't yet forged a strong bond with his mother. Unlike other four-year-old boys who are eager to explore their father's world, take care of themselves, and make friends, he is concerned about being forgotten or left out. He senses that closeness to others will meet his needs, but his bond with mother is not strong enough to bring satisfaction or security. For him weaning will feel like further abandonment and rejection. As he grows up he will continue a desperate search for connection. He will fear being abandoned and rejected by women. He will fear his own needs. This is the man who will do anything for the love of a woman, yet never find her love to be enough. Rather than become the autonomous person Erikson describes in his second crisis, he develops shame and doubt about his existence, needs, and efforts.

It is this early lack of connection with his mother that produces frantic men. This is a crucial time without which the boy will begin a sporadic, frantic search for connection with someone or something. Someone needs to be interested in who he is. Someone *has* to be interested in defining who he is. That special someone must find him interesting and approve of him.

A woman once told me, "You know, it is the easiest thing in the world to get a man, all you have to do is act interested in him. You can have your pick."

An actor candidly told me, "I just can't resist it when a woman is attracted to me. I have to have that love. I can't turn it down." As a result of his failure to turn down any woman's attention, he has lost several important relationships and gotten a venereal disease. He has looked frantically through life for a connection that would tell him he is good, valuable, and interesting. He is still trying to find a connection with a woman that will let him nurse contentedly and take in the sustenance he has always needed. Without a healing deep in his soul, he will never be able to give up his frantic search.

This helps us understand why the typical sexual fantasy of men can be reduced to this: he finds a woman who goes crazy over him and can't get enough of him. While there are many variations and exceptions, this one remains the prototype. Tragically, many men have sexualized their need for connectedness. Men who are attracted to pornography, for example, should consider that they may lack a connection with someone who will tell them who they really are—someone who is eager to be with them. Such a man might think that his highest glory would come from having a woman go nuts over him. He has a deep wound that needs to be healed before he can begin to regain control of his life. Sex will not heal that wound, for as nice as it might be to have a woman who is crazy about you, it cannot replace a mother or the Creator who is delighted to know you just the way you are.

The prophet Isaiah once wrote, "Can a mother forget the baby at her breast and have no compassion on the child she has borne? Though she may forget, I will not forget you!" (Is 49:15). To get stuck in this early stage and replace the interest of a God who loves us like a mother nursing her child with unconnected sexual passion is like eating the charcoal briquets instead of the barbecued steak. It is close, it is hot, but it does not satisfy.

This frantic search for connectedness can lie behind family dysfunctions and even religious addictions. People tied to "toxic faith" often try desperately to do anything they can for God's love and attention, as though we needed to do anything in order to receive God's love.

The boy who hasn't forged a bond with his mother senses this desperate need to be connected and lets it be known in various ways. This is usually obvious to adults who say correctly,

"He is just looking for attention." Attention is exactly what he craves. If he has not been taught how he can meet his needs by asking for what he needs, then he hopes that by getting attention from his mother or someone else he will find what he needs. Usually, however, the boy does not even understand that his search for attention is a request. Remember that the crying child has to be taught his cry is a request, or he will not even recognize that fact. The child seeking attention has not learned to ask for what he needs. He is not ready for weaning, his second great passage.

Not all the bonds between mother and child are good. In fact, bonds can be generally sorted into two types. Both types of bonds bring closeness between mother and child and serve to meet needs, but there the similarities end. Both fear and love can bond us to others. Fear and love can motivate our behavior. Fear and love are antagonists to each other. Fear and love can even produce similar behavior. But in the case of a mother-and-son bond, fear produces defective connections.

Love allows us to see the other person for who he or she is. Contrary to the popular expression, love is not blind. To be a good mother to the unweaned child, a mother must accurately sense the child's feelings and needs and put words and actions to them. Her child will then feel known, understood, and cared for. When the bond between mother and child is based on fear, then the mother can no longer see the boy and his needs clearly. She wraps him up in a blanket and feigns care in other ways because she is afraid of what other mothers will think of her. She keeps him from exploring because she is afraid he will hurt himself. She feeds him because she is afraid he will get sick or grouchy. She hushes his crying because she fears others will think she is a bad mother. As a result the boy does not learn his needs and does not trust his feelings. He learns his mother's fears instead. For such a boy, life becomes a long-term effort to keep people from becoming upset or afraid.

When bonds are based on fears, there is no way that weaning or any other stage of growth can go right. The boy raised on fear will not know his own needs and feelings clearly. If mother's fears are fairly realistic, then he will cope well with life; if her fears are exotic and irrational he will have little chance of discovering who he really is.

When an unweaned boy has a close bond with his mother, she will appear and help him every time something bad happens. From this he learns that bad things bring closeness and comfort. He need not fear bad events or feelings as he is not alone. Confidence, hope, and faith are built from this simple foundation. This basic trust is the foundation which is built in his first year of life, relating back to Erikson's first crisis. Consider the confidence of the man who knows in his gut that something which is bad is but the precursor of the good if he remains faithful. Such a man is not easily swayed from his path by adversity or pain. The security of his bond with his mother serves as an anchor. This is the reason that bonds based on fear don't work well. These bonds are always at risk to any fear greater than the fear that bonds.

The stronger the bond of love between mother and son, the more secure will be his anchor. The stronger his bond with mother, the greater will be his capacity to bond with the world around him. Knowing he will not be pulled away from mother's love, he can hold on to wild things and risk what other boys and men would be afraid of. More importantly, these boys will not fear those they love and try to control them. The less he needs to control others the larger a boy's world can become. With a strong love-bond to his mother, a boy can risk involvement without trying to control others, because even if he is hurt he knows that hurt will soon be followed by closeness, comfort, and healing.

In boys this anchor can best be seen in the way a boy forms friends. Well anchored children are usually invited to play by others and allow other children to join in their play. Poorly anchored children beg to join other children. They are often rejected and end up playing alone. When they do succeed in playing with others, they are frequently displaced or reject any additional playmates who want to join. Billy was this way. When he had a friend his most common words to others were, "You can't play with us."

A true bond of love is characterized by appreciation, encouragement, independence, creativity, and the ability to risk. The bond of fear by contrast is built of control, anger, threats, shame, rigidity, rejection, or clinging. As with most of life, nothing is perfect. There are few perfect bonds of love or fear. Since love is stronger than fear, it sinks deeper into the soul. A little love will produce a bond that is easily overcome by fear. Strong love will withstand great fear before giving way. Fear stretches love as though it were a rubber band. If the fear proves too strong, the love snaps and fear takes over. This is tremendously confusing to the boy with a fearful mother and discouraging to such a mother who wishes to love her son.

Perhaps love is only as strong as the weakest bond. A mother whose own security is not strongly anchored in love will quickly be overcome by fear. The frightened or angry mother will not be able to sustain the pressure of the fears inside her and will snap from love to fear as her own sense of being threatened grows.

Karin loved her children. She hugged them, fed them, played with them, shared them with her adoring husband. She appeared to be all a mommy could be for the unweaned child. But Karin had a flaw, a rather deep fear of rejection, which she pushed aside. True, she loved her husband and children and they loved her. When everyone was loving or even sad, she was the mom of moms. But every once in a while Karin would "lose it" with her son Justin. She was always very sorry for it afterwards, but she just couldn't take it when he refused to do what she told him and ignored her. She would respond by yelling at him and even shook him a couple of times. But that scared her so she stopped. Justin's unresponsiveness awakened in Karin the fear she always carried that her father's unresponsiveness meant he did not love her. This fear led her to try and scare a response out of Justin. This reliance on fear to connect with her son is the bond of fear with her father being played out again with her son. Deep inside, Karin really believes it is fear that connects parents with their children. It is reflected in how she acts.

One function of a good mother is to notice her son's growth. She does not just pay attention to what he needs to be safe, full, and warm. The good mother watches her son grow and change. It is by watching what comes out of him that she appreciates his uniqueness. In time her appreciation will become his as well because for now the unweaned boy does not know that he is unique. This develops the autonomy needed for him to resolve the second crisis Erikson describes.

Indeed, what a close intimate world surrounds the baby boy. It is a world made for him to the best of his parents' abilities. It is a place so intimate that we must take our feelings by the hand just to look inside. It is a world of touching and sensing, of knowing and loving, and once in a while, of holding our noses. But as each day passes the boy learns to ask and receive. He learns who to ask and how to say it well, "Go ask Daddy to tie your shoes," says Mommy. "Do you want more pureed peas?" or, "How's my pumpkin today?" all herald a passage to a world of questions and answers. The boy is preparing to be weaned and can start to stand on his own.

We will study weaning more carefully in the next chapter about a boy and his father since this process depends greatly on Dad for its ultimate success. The boy learns who he is in the confluence of many people in which he is both separate and yet joined to others. For now, however, the boy enters into a major passage in his life. His mother, the rock of his security, begins to change. No longer does she always come at his call or even know what is wrong. These days her words are, "Tell me what you want," or, "What is wrong?" or even, "You'll have to wait until dinner."

MOTHER AND THE WEANED SON

With Mother's excellent help, a boy comes to find out that he can need, feel, ask, and receive. What a wonderful world this has turned out to be, a world where he can take initiative without having to feel guilt for trying. As he learns to ask more clearly, the day of weaning approaches when the boy must make his first stand alone in the world. Weaning marks the time when the boy is officially on his own. As I said earlier, weaning in the sense I am using it, involves a whole set of behaviors and attitudes whereby a boy begins to separate from the mother and achieve a basic level of independence. Mother is no longer in charge of guessing what the weaned boy asks her for. The boy must now ask for himself. Not asking will bring with it not receiving, for Mother is no longer in charge of guessing what is on his mind. Sure, he can solicit help, but even that is now largely up to him. With Mother's help, he has learned to put words to his needs and feelings so that others can know him without having to read his mind. This is the first major achievement of childhood.

The well-bonded mother has her hands full with the weaned boy at first. It is not easy to build confidence that requests will be heard. The newly weaned boy is like the child with new skates or a bicycle. Some just take off while others must carefully test each step. But whether it is through encouraging or trying to keep up, Mother helps the weaned child to become successful at his new stage of independence.

After he has had a successful start, his mother will steadily demand more from the boy. He will learn to ask correctly, at the right time, to the right person. Soon he will be busy learning about his rapidly expanding world. As his perceptions allow more complexity, his requests will become more complex. Before long he must begin to calculate time into his requests. This begins to pave the way for becoming a part of history as a man. To do so he must figure out ahead of time that he will become hungry and how much he will want to eat before he packs his lunch. Mother helps greatly in teaching the boy how to manage his time, such as getting his boots and coat on before the school bus arrives.

If his mother is not ready to let him grow past weaning, then there may be endless fights about wearing jackets, boots, or what to eat and when to do something. The weaned boy needs his mother to watch his development and help him stay in the range of manageable mistakes. Particularly if the mother relates to her son through her own fears, she will have trouble allowing him to learn from his own mistakes. Sometimes, a mother tries to keep her son unweaned by continuing to be his voice. Such a mother tells the world how to understand her son's feelings, reactions, actions, and needs. Not uncommonly this sort of mother soon makes a career of cleaning up the messes her son has made.

On the other hand, a boy likes his mother because she keeps the world "soft" when each day it becomes increasingly hard. When his mother continues to be a stable source of warmth and care, the boy is free to try harder efforts, knowing that he has an anchor of comfort and acceptance. A mother's special gifts of knowing him, which previously helped her know his diapers were wet or messy, now help him know that he is interesting. Mother helps him remember those early lessons about his value, just because he is her son, not because of anything he can do. As a result the boy continues to share the wider world he is discovering with his mother.

Not everyone makes the transition through weaning successfully. Some poor souls never reach this second passage with an adequate foundation. They spend the rest of their unhappy lives looking for someone who will read their minds, know what they need, and do it for them without their having to ask. Often these frustrated and unfulfilled men mistake this kind of care for love. Worse yet, they feel unloved if others do not guess what they want without having to ask. "If I have to tell them or ask for something it doesn't count," they say. These sad people never made it through weaning. They still want love the way an unweaned child does.

In some ways we could describe the dysfunctional family as one in which members who are old enough to feed themselves are trying to get the rest of the family (or even particular members) to act like an infant's mother to them. A father, for instance, might expect his wife, or even his children, to guess what he wants without his having to ask. A little grunt, a turn of the head, or a tug at his coffee cup means he wants more coffee; and "Mother," whoever she is, must jump to meet her baby's needs. How very much those actions resemble the unweaned child's cries, turning his head towards his mother's breast or tugging on her blouse for his supper. If the immature father's needs are not met, like those of a baby, he then believes he has a grievance—proof that he was not loved in the way that every nursing boy requires.

Men who were weaned without learning how to meet their own needs through asking and receiving will often react to breasts as though they were some extraordinarily good thing. This ultimately has nothing to do with whether the boy was breast-fed or bottle-fed. Surviving the passage through weaning is based on the boy's solid bond with his mother and her training him to express his needs and feelings in appropriate words and actions by the time he is four and ready to be weaned from mother. Not uncommonly, such men have a fascination with breasts, particularly big ones.

Now, indeed, breasts are an extraordinarily good thing if we consider the wonder of how a woman's body becomes a fountain of life, flowing with enough milk to sustain life and promote tremendous growth. That is amazing, but such is not the fascination of the improperly weaned boy. To him breasts are a good object beyond his reach—a treasure cruelly kept from him by the powerful creatures that have them. Breasts are objects to be desired, looked for, and stared at in a ceaseless fantasy to have them all.

How to get access to breasts can be an obsession with some men. There is no shortage of lingerie and clothing manufacturers willing to exploit the man who does not know what he really needs. He will pay through the nose for the things that do not satisfy and wonder what is wrong with him.

Girls who do not make it through weaning with the proper

preparation to meet their own needs by asking and receiving also develop their own fascination for breasts. However, since God endowed them with their own set, the girl's preoccupation is different from the boy's. Girls wonder about the sufficiency of their own supply. This sufficiency is usually measured by attractiveness and the current fashions. For the improperly weaned girl, displaying and simultaneously hiding her breasts becomes an obsession. Endless shaping, padding, covering with lace, selecting attractive necklines, finding just the right tightness for blouses, choosing seductive styles of bathing suits and sleepwear, all become part of the quest for the perfect buxom figure. Surgeons can be found to add their modifications if clothing and padding do not suffice.

If, by some chance, an improperly weaned man and woman should meet, the resulting interaction gets physical rather quickly. Even if no touching happens between the two, the woman displays her attractions to a man who works to possess them in some way, either by seeing more or getting closer—much as an unhappily weaned child would try to get to his mother's supply. Meanwhile, the woman tries to keep the man's attentions while staying out of reach, acting out her own interpretation of her mother's distancing after weaning.

The weaned boy who does not know how to meet his needs by asking will quickly become angry. Unmet needs produce anger, and since no one likes an angry boy, the frustration soon escalates as his anger triggers increasing rejection from others. The mocking phrase "He just wants attention" is usually close behind, leaving him even angrier and disenfranchised—a casualty of the second passage.

MOTHER AND THE MAN

My wife Kitty went down to pick up our older son Jamie from college. It was the end of exam week for both of them, since Kitty had started back to college to learn sign language. As they settled in for the two-hour drive home, my son said, "It's good to have you to myself all the way home. There are some things I want to talk to you about." Kitty was delighted. They went on to talk about girls, dating, surpassing one's own parents, and many other things.

Young men need to know whether they should fear the new power they have discovered within themselves. They instinctively turn to their mothers to see if they are securely anchored. Does Mom still find them lovable, or is she afraid of their newfound intellect, body, and skills? She is also a valuable keeper of her son's history. As each man tries to see himself as he is, he must look through his mother's eyes to find out what he was like before he could really observe himself. After screening out the things that Mom always says, he finds consolation and hope that his mother found him interesting, lovable, and special even before he could do all the marvelous things he does now. It is almost embarrassing to think that he was once as helpless as Mom describes, when she alone understood his beginning efforts at language and he called sugar "oogo."

Now that he is a man and must begin to deal fairly with others, he has his first real chance to admire his mother's ability to know what someone else could feel. This ability to sense what others feel helps him bridge the gap to people whose worlds are different than his own. At the same time, it takes him back to his earliest days of life when mother's attentiveness first broke through the borders of his own existence. Like his mother, he now breaks into the borders of other people's worlds—now a blushing girl, then an irritable boss, or then again, a friend who has withdrawn and needs his sympathy. Like his good mother, he enters this scary new world seeking to keep it intact and yet change it because he took the time to know it.

Mother's encouragement means so much at these times. Her faith that he can successfully negotiate these barriers, even if he is far less skilled than she, brings the hope that he can touch others' worlds and be touched in return. The man who lacks this ability will find himself alone no matter how many friends he appears to have or how often he gets someone in bed.

MOTHER FOR HER GROWN SON,
THE FATHER OR ELDER

Mother-and-son relationships continue to be important throughout the son's lifetime. It is interesting that Jesus gave his mother into the care of St. John the Beloved when he was old enough to be a father. Later on, we read that the apostle Paul, who was definitely an elder, had been adopted by Rufus' mother who was like a mother to him. This he found very precious. Perhaps the man who had learned to be content in any situation liked someone to worry if his soup was still hot and if his tunic didn't need a little mending. We are never so old that we lose the appreciation for someone with the ability to see us and love what they see.

One of the things that impressed me the most about my dad as a child was his relationship to his mother. Even as a busy missionary for over twenty-five years, my dad wrote to his mother every week. Every week she would write back. Almost all of her letters ended with, "Well, I see the mailman coming now, so I'd better get this in the mailbox." These words brought a picture to my dad's mind of the little house he had helped build on 422 Bauman Road with lilacs in front and his mother sitting by the window. In the countryside of Colombia, torn by hatred and civil war, amidst constant threats, he was reminded that he was lovable and worth protecting. So it was that his mother reminded him of how God saw him, even though she probably did not know that was what she was doing.

Mothers are at their best when they can see their son for who he is in God's sight and in his own historical context. Mary kept all the things she heard about Jesus in her heart. This is what a mother does, she keeps the things about her children deep in her heart and she treasures them. One young man recently got angry and beat up his fiancée, whereupon she promptly broke off the engagement. When the young man returned to his mother, he said, "I just can't believe I did that!" His mother wisely began at the beginning and reminded him that this was not the first female he had hit. From there she told him who he had been, even back to his childhood. She was indeed a good mother, for she told him not only his history but also who he was beneath the violence—a scared boy who needed help he could not give to himself.

WHEN YOUR MOTHER IS DEAD

There are two ways a mother can die. The most obvious death is physical. Once a man's mother has died physically he can only remember her words and actions, and it is important to do exactly that. Proverbs, chapter 31 contains the sayings that King Lemuel learned from his mother. Included among them is training on how to rule and marry wisely. She helps him to see what he really needs among all the options open to a king. "The women who make eyes at kings are not good for you," she tells him in effect, "look for a capable woman." She shares with him her ability as a mother to sense what is really needed by telling Lemuel to speak up for the dumb, the wretched, the embittered, and the poor. The king did well to remember his mother's words about who he was and what he really needed. History had made him king, and Scripture still contains his mother's sayings for us to remember. So just as mothers are to remember their children's history, so sons are to remember their mothers and treasure them in their hearts.

There is another form of death which is far worse than the physical and much more insidious. Mothers and fathers who die this way still walk around and talk to their sons. These relationships are like marriages which are dead, but the paperwork continues. These mother-and-son relationships are dead, but the facade continues to stand, especially during the holidays. Such a relationship is death-dealing to the son. If a man comes to realize that his mother cannot see who he is in God's eyes, he is badly in need of adoption by a godly mother. Because she holds our history, a mother reminds us of who we are and how we are connected to others. Adoptive mothers, while they hold less of our history, may well be gifted with more vision about what we are actually like inside. Like the apostle Paul, who treasured his adoptive mother, we should not be afraid of adoption. If a man like Paul needed an adoptive mother, then all of us could benefit from one too.

Now let us turn to the boy and his father. When exactly does this bond begin to develop between father and son? What exactly happens when this bond is not strong and healthy?

THREE

A Boy and His Father

The child grew and was weaned, and on the day Isaac was weaned Abraham held a great feast. **Genesis 21:8**

FORMING THE BOND WITH FATHER

W HEN MY FIRST SON WAS BORN, I was elated to be a witness to something as marvelous as the ushering in of a new life. A few fathers had been allowed into the delivery room in that hospital by then, but they were kept off in a corner. The doctor took the radical step of allowing me to be close to the action after a very careful screening. This was to be my first child, and I wanted to know everything about him or her. Anticipation was intense as I waited to meet and appreciate the life I had helped form.

My son had made his first passage successfully by late afternoon. As I called all the relatives to tell them the news, the question was asked time after time, "How are the mother and baby?" I began to wonder where the father fit in. It got worse from there. I awoke one night from a dead sleep to find myself being rolled over the edge of the bed and onto the floor. My wife had awakened and, after failing to find the baby, concluded that I must be lying on him. That got me the quick trip to the floor. Then she remembered that the baby was back in his crib.

Breast-feeding did nothing to help me find out what a father was for, except that Kitty took all my handkerchiefs and used them to catch drips. At first I felt that picking up the baby was like handling high explosives. Any quick motion might set something off, and dropping it would be disaster. Buckets of advice from the ladies around me did not build confidence either. One aunt gave the play-by-play and another gave the color commentary. "Look at the way he holds the head. Not like that! Here, let me show you." "Men!" said the other, "don't they know a baby won't break?" Well, if they don't break, then what was wrong with how I held his head, I wondered, and what is a father for?

Let me tell you what dads are for. Dad will throw him up in the air and catch him again. Together they will bounce, run, race and even strain themselves, from time to time. Together they find expression for the life that the boy has received from his mother. In time the boy will learn that life comes from the father as well, but it is in a different form.

Appreciation, anticipation, holding, comfort, and play are some of the first gifts a son receives from his father. These activities produce a bond between the father and his son that will grow and enrich both of their lives.

EXPERIENCING THE BOND WITH FATHER

Dad meanwhile has formed a special connection with this child. When you think about it, this alone is a remarkable event. Unlike mother, who risked her life just to give birth to him, who carried him inside her for nine months, who fed him from her body, slept with him, and sensed his needs and feelings, Dad must bond because someone said to him, "Behold your child."

Not only so, but the average American father must overcome some resentment he carries towards the child who has taken his wife's attention and affection away from him. (In cultures where men do not depend so exclusively on their wives to meet all their emotional needs, there is less of a crisis for men when Mamma has a baby.) Still, because the father feels that he has and must give life, a power beyond his own pushes him to bond with his son.

The boy's first connections to his mother surround him and engulf him. He connects to her by taking her breast in his mouth, but Dad *must not* engulf him or go into him. Dad moves him up and down and throws him in the air. Dad connects and disconnects. Dad puts demands on his body. Dad is the place Mom tells him to try to walk to with his first steps. With Dad he must be his own person. Dad richly appreciates each thing that makes the boy his own person. Without Dad's help, Mother might well become the whole world. Dad soon becomes proof that Mom can't understand everyone all the time, and Mom becomes proof that Dad, for all his power, can't move everything. Through Dad he can see that there is no need to be afraid of being connected to Mother. Dad's eagerness to be with her and even compete with his son for her attention give proof of this.

Furthermore, the boy need not fear his mother (and after her all women) will control him or overpower his weak efforts at becoming an individual. His connection with Dad lets him be different than Mom and yet appreciated and admired. The boy can then treasure closeness without fear and seek independence with enthusiasm. Dad is a bridge to the wider world who will help the boy know the meaning of his efforts and the meaning of the world's effects on him.

The baby boy who discovers his dad discovers a wonderful thing. This creature is the one his mother, the source of life, waits and looks for. He is harder, hairier, and usually bigger than Mom. He appears and disappears in an almost random way. Dad represents the unpredictable, the exciting, the one who brings change. Being up on Daddy's shoulders is like riding an elephant or driving a fast car. It is awesome how much power the boy can control and direct. It is here the boy begins to learn of meekness.

The story is told of a Greek general with Alexander the Great who wrote home about his new war horse. It was, he said, the strongest horse he had ever had. The beast would run almost tirelessly and yet it was guided by the lightest touch, a truly meek horse. Wrestling with Dad, or riding on his back, wrapping little arms around his head and nearly poking out his eyes, the boy begins to learn of meekness. To him, Dad is great power under sensitive control. This is autonomy—Erickson's second crisis—without shame and doubt. It teaches the boy to use his will wisely by imitating his father's wisdom.

Just as the boy needs a breast to receive life, so the boy needs a body of his own to experience that life. Dad, the chap with a body most like his own, is there to help the boy learn to live in his body. And whether or not the aunts think highly of how these two start out bridging the gap in their body size, it is Dad who is best equipped to show the boy what he can do. To discover the boy's body and mind, they will play and work together. They will explore his endurance, strength, creativity, and abilities. It is said that when Bach would sit down at a new organ he would take it to the limits and see what sort of "lungs" it had. Dads do that. Together he and his boy will explore and expand the limits of his world. With Dad the boy will come into full possession of his body and mind. Together they will play. They don't have to test the limits, they just want to.

The boy's bond with his father teaches him self-expression, how to play, work, make things change, and influence his environment. This is the beginning of the initiative he must show between ages three and six, Erikson's third crisis. He needs two influences. Not only is he the sort of person Mom taught him to see with needs and feelings who can take things in, but he can also make a change in the world around him. He can do things and make things happen. Even before weaning this fatherly influence begins to pull a richer variety of expression out of the boy.

Dad is very interested in what abilities the boy has inside of himself and wants to try them out. Together they see if he can catch a ball, ride a bike, drive the car while sitting on Dad's lap, or shoot a slingshot.

Around Dad things are always going wrong. The boy learns that Dad smiles when he tries and misses. Together they can laugh at mistakes. Together they test the limits to see what is possible today. Together he learns to stretch his limits but to have limits as well, for he can clearly see the difference in power between himself and his dad. He can't do everything Dad can—not yet.

Just as the mother cleared the way for the boy to know what he needed and felt because she was not afraid of his feelings or demands, the father helps the boy to grow past his fears of what he can do. When the boy is afraid or in a rage, or even in pain, his father's assuring closeness lets him know that it will be okay.

So it is that the boy learns what he can do as well as his limitations. He learns to receive and to create. He also learns that he has great value. What he takes in does not give him value and what he makes happen does not give him value. He doesn't do these things to get value or love, they are just part of who he is. His connections with Mom and Dad let him know his value.

Dad is the model for the little boy. As weaning approaches, Dad becomes a larger player in the boy's life. Not only has Mother been teaching him how to ask for what he needs, but most often he has been able to practice on Dad. Many times the results are remarkable. Not only does Dad respond when asked, but when they explore the world together Dad gets similar results from other people. What a wonderful world for the boy. He knows that this enormous person is what he will be like when he is big. Just following the future around is fascinating.

Boys learn much from their mothers and fathers, but they practice what they learn with their siblings and peers. As you would expect, they compare lessons with each other as well as practicing. The influence of these practice sessions is considerable on every child's development. Parents who supervise these practice sessions well will find that they produce a strengthening of the lessons they have taught. But unexamined or unregulated play can often teach very different lessons to the boy about who he is or what he can do. The good father is attentive to this possibility and reviews his lessons frequently with his son.

Each member of the family exerts his or her influence. Individual uniqueness prevents us from making accurate generalizations about each family member's role, but some generalizations about mothers and fathers will help us divide the work of parenting according to who might be better at a given task. This difference between a mother and a father is in some ways a difference in emphasis. Single parents can do most everything themselves, particularly if they recruit other people to be surrogate parents for their children. No child with only one father has enough fathers. A father's duty is to secure additional fathers for his son. In so doing, the good father helps his son move towards the community of men and become someone greater than himself. By taking in the diversity of different men's fathering abilities, a boy will grow past his father's limitations and blind spots much more readily.

A father may not be less intuitive than a mother. It is not that fathers totally lack the capacity to sense what a child is feeling and what they need. Fathers can provide these functions quite well if they will take the time. Time is the critical factor. Babies don't leave that much time. We still laugh at my wife's idea when our first child was born that when she stayed home to be with him, she would have time for projects she had always wanted to do around the house.

No, time is scarce and men usually lose their intuition and sensitivity if they are doing more than one activity at the same time. The most intuitive man will usually become oblivious to others if he is trying to sort the mail, cook a meal, or plan his day. Women, on the other hand, can usually do these tasks and still maintain their sensitivity. Consequently a mother can usually wash the dishes and watch the kids, while Dad can only manage one or the other. Although men and women can each do almost all the same things the other can, no man will be a mother and no woman a father.

THE WEANING BOND

Dad is also very important in helping a boy meet his needs. This becomes the focus of his father's training once the day of weaning arrives. Weaning is the first major achievement that mother, father, and child reach as a family team, and what an achievement it is.

Weaning is the second great passage in a child's life. In more traditional cultures, it is a specific time when breast-feeding stops, but its significance is the boy's readiness to feed and care for himself. It begins to happen when he no longer wants his baby bottle, holds his own spoon, puts on his clothes by himself, and gets into bed on his own. These are all parts of weaning in the sense that I am using the word. Unfortunately, we tend to rush them all, rather than treasuring them by celebrating these milestones with family and friends. Yet there is no reason not to enjoy and celebrate each part of weaning. They are all part of our son's history.

When Isaac was weaned Abraham held a feast. The day of his son's weaning was community news and everyone was invited. It was the boy's introduction to his community and their introduction to the boy. The feast made it clear that this boy was important, under his father's care and protection, and in need of the community's involvement. The feast let everyone know that while the boy had depended on his mother until then, his father was now in charge of his nutrition. Even as his mother brought him into the world through her labor, the father now brought him into the world surrounded by the fruit of his labor.

The boy began to learn again what he needed from others and how to ask for it. For the boy it meant that he was now able to feed himself and everyone was happy about this achievement. At the feast there was plenty of food to help him learn. He was one of the people now and past his first major hurdle thanks to his mother's excellent training. A boy who could feed himself was ready for bigger adventures, and everyone rejoiced. He also learned that he did not feed himself in isolation. A feast meant that all those with him also celebrated and rejoiced that they too could feed themselves.

Weaning is Dad's day in much the same way that the birth day is Mother's day. Neither day would come to be without the other's efforts, but special changes take place in a boy's life that day that involve each parent in unique ways. Comforted by his father's voice and surrounded by his father's ample supply, the boy who can feed himself is now ready to learn many new ways to meet his needs. Buying, growing, building, finding, stalking, thinking, gathering, chasing, and waiting are all ways that his father meets his needs, and soon they will be learned by the boy as well.

So it is, if all goes well, that the boy will learn to "take in" energy from his mother and to "put out" energy from his father. At weaning the father's role begins in earnest as he takes the boy into the wider world. Each trip goes farther from Mother's storehouse of supplies, but with Dad's help the boy discovers new sources.

Each adventure with Dad starts with leaving home and ends with a return to rest. The boy learns that both leaving and returning are good. Connecting and disconnecting in endless succession, yet with no more fear than he felt releasing his hold on his mother's breast, the boy sets out to learn who he really is. Soon, having learned how it is done, he will launch on his own adventures in the care of his watchful community, for his community has been prepared by his father to receive him.

This process is a stress on the father, just as teaching the boy to ask for his needs was a stress to his mother. The father's desire to see his son grow and to enjoy his boy provide the motivation to overcome this strain. Fathers who train their sons out of fear push them to perform and achieve, rather than teaching them to explore, express themselves, and find satisfaction in life.

Through this maze of confusion, it is the father who guides his son to satisfaction. Mother was much easier on this score for her milk was always satisfying (unless she ate certain things), but the choices are not all good when a boy must decide what to feed himself. Does he choose chocolate chip cookies or broccoli, potatoes or zucchini, eggs or liver, juice or cola? In what order?

Learning about food is just the beginning of choosing between options. What clothes should he wear, what friends should he choose, what activities should he spend his playtime doing? What is worth effort, suffering, or pain to obtain? What should be turned down even if it is immediately pleasurable because it is not satisfying? Father is the one who, through finding out what really satisfies in life, can guide his steps and choices. In time his father will show him the difference between pleasure and satisfaction, and in so doing the boy will learn wisdom.

WHEN THINGS GO WRONG

We can better understand the importance of a boy's bonds with his father when we look at what happens if they are missing or defective. No bond to father leaves the boy adrift with himself and adrift in the world of men. The man who is unconnected with his father does not trust other men. He does not trust his wife or daughter with other men either.

The man who is not connected with his father is at great risk of becoming a conformist. He does not know how to be separate and make things happen. He is more prone to change than to cause changes. He is not in full possession of his own body. This makes it harder to go out and do what needs doing. Dad is the one who teaches us to go after what we want and make things happen.

A weak bond with Dad produces a frantic search for control, power, and freedom. Such men need to get away from what they fear will control them. This kind of man fears commitment, challenge, work, and struggle. It doesn't matter who gets hurt as he tries to escape. Rather than the connection to his father that tells him he can make things happen, there is fear which leads to running away. Escape is necessary when strength is missing—strength to get involved and stay involved. Men run away to work, sports, and study. Some have made minor careers out of trying to be free of any responsibilities in life.

God as our Father says, "When you have done everything, stand." We don't have to run. He promises us the strength. We can go, we can do, we can be what is needed—we don't need to run. There need be no frantic search for freedom. Jesus did not run around saying, "Let me out of here, these people are trying to run my life."

I get that way sometimes. I remember one time a family fight broke out on an old subject. I quickly decided to go to the back bedroom to pray. It was the perfect cover. I would gladly have prayed until everything was better, and I could go back out safely. God didn't like my using him to escape my role and responsibility, so before long it became time to take a stand. I don't know that we resolved anything that day, but God prevailed in saying I could take the heat.

Not only is the missing father a problem, but at times a father will fail to be a good model. Each boy is the closest replica on earth of what his father is like. How he feels about his father will have a huge impact on how he sees himself. Even in trying to be very different from his father, the boy is not free from the powerful influence of these feelings.

If a large oak tree drops an acorn which grows into another oak tree, it will be the closest replica of the original tree that we can find. Still the effects of climate, lighting, wind, and disease may cause the two trees to grow very differently. In that sense the boy can be the closest replica of who his father was created to be, although through the effects of his own climate he may grow in very different ways.

God didn't create any trash. We trash ourselves and get trashed because there is evil in the world. But even if your father was the worst father in the world, that is not how his life was supposed to grow. To see him through the eyes of heaven, we see an oak tree that never grew up right. The lightning strike of '37 and the winter of '52 took their toll. The seed of the oak tree need not grow that way.

If then we totally reject our fathers, we reject the model on which we were based. Such a rejection is a rejection of our very selves. Somewhere in there we get tripped up. Until we can see our fathers through the eyes of heaven and see which parts of Dad are the distortions of evil and what is the created order, we cannot see ourselves correctly either.

If someone were in a car accident and went through the windshield, we would not assume that what we found was what their face should look like. We can figure that out because we know what faces should look like, but we don't really know what evil does to people's souls, especially when we grow up with them. That face we saw on our father we took to be normal. We could not tell what the scars were unless our father was honest with us about his history. The truth comes from looking at that history through the eyes of heaven.

To look at injured people with understanding we must know what they were before the injury. People with faces full of glass from the windshield will rightfully see themselves as ugly, but are they ugly? First we must take the glass out and stitch up their faces.

To stretch this analogy a bit, all of us have had our faces jammed through the windshield of sin and the world. We need our faces reconstructed by someone who knows what they should look like to begin with. A plastic surgeon would want a "before" picture. But since our world is thousands of years into the wreck, we have to go back to the Creator for a "before" picture. We can no longer determine whether our faces should look as they do, or if what we see is the result of going through the windshield of sin. We ask our heavenly Father to pick the glass out and reconstruct our face so that it looks like our father, the way our father was meant to look. In doing this we must come to terms with the fact that our father has gone through the windshield. His face has been crushed, and cleaning up his face is God's business, not ours. Often a father has marred his son's face with the same shards of glass to make him look like himself. Many a son has undertaken to put the glass right back into his father's face to show him what it feels like.

At one point in my training when I was being instructed in behavior modification, my services were requested to help a boy who was not doing well in school. We set up a program of goals he could reach. In return he received certain rewards. The reward the boy requested was to spend some time with his dad doing something fun. The father agreed and the standards for success were set. As a result the boy began to apply himself diligently to his studies and earned all his points.

Two weeks later the family came in. The boy was worse than ever, so I asked what went wrong. The boy said, "I did everything, but my dad would not spend time with me."

I asked his father if this were true and he said, "Hey! That is how the world is! You don't always get what you expect. The kid just has to learn to live with that." The dad was happy, he had just taught his son a valuable lesson—what it is like to have your face put through the windshield of life. Now his face would look like his father's. This is how he saw being a good father. He needed to teach certain lessons and get the glass arranged in his son's face the way it had been in his own. This is what happens when you don't have the eyes of heaven to see what someone ought to look like.

This father was, as far as I could determine, well intentioned. There is a lot of training that occurs this way by those who don't know how a face ought to look. Deep inside men sense something wrong with the ways they relate to their children. And yet, without the courage to face their own pain and their own losses, the trickle-down of cruelty is inevitable. Men, particularly those of this generation, must face the fact that the mentors, fathers, elders, and role models that they seek are usually not available. For this generation the first and last step of grief will be learning to give what they have never received. It is the first step because unless we give, we will not grieve deeply. It is the last because when we have grieved our losses, we will have life to give.

FATHERS OF MEN

It makes me a little uncomfortable to say so, but there have been times when my marriage got a little bumpy. Perhaps you know what I mean when I say that and if you do then bless you. Some bumps have lasted more then a few hours or even a few days. It was on one of those occasions that I called my dad. He, in his great wisdom, reminded me of my original intentions in marrying my wife.

I remember well the day that my dad first asked me about my intentions in marrying. He asked me why I wanted to get married as, in his opinion and that of the state of Minnesota, I was a bit young. Did I know, he inquired, of the difficulties inherent in my selection of a mate? As we walked through the park at the edge of Lake Bemidji and glanced at the paintings of the local artists, we reviewed my life—past, present and future. Now, over the phone and fifteen years later he took me back to that park, the site of our talk. "You knew there would be tough times when you got married," he said, "And I seem to recall that you wanted the challenge." He was right and reminded me of Superchicken's words to Fred, "You knew the job was dangerous when you took it!"

But my father's compassion was deeper than it appeared at first, and we talked at some length about what it means to do things that strain and even hurt at times. Even though he did not particularly agree with me or support all that I was doing, my dad reminded me of my history, my commitments and, most importantly, that there wasn't anything unmanly about pain.

In later chapters we will learn more about a man and his father and even what to do if your father is dead either physically or in other ways. A man's connection to his father goes on long beyond his father's death. Jesus taught that it was not what goes into a man that makes him unclean but what comes out of his heart and mouth. A wise father will try to bring the best out of us, for he can see with the eyes of heaven what there is inside of us waiting to come out. We do well to return often to his words and remember them.

But what happens when a man has never learned what it means to be a boy—when the care and development that should have been provided by his parents has short-circuited? We explore this problem, which is all too common, in our next chapter.

FOUR

The Man Who
Has Never Been a Boy

LARRY HAD THE NICEST HOUSE on the street. It wasn't the most expensive house, but everything about it was as close to perfect as Larry could get it. He worked on it at least four hours a night and twelve to sixteen hours a day on weekends. He had been working this way for almost six years and, as he said, it was "coming along." The carpet, paint, moldings, garden, grass, wiring, windows, water heater, shelves, garage, retaining wall, fruit trees, sinks, counter top, and dog run were among the improvements Larry had made.

Larry felt self-conscious about his results. The neighbors teased him a bit, and his wife still seemed unhappy with his results, so he could not decide whether to work more or work less. Larry had a bad case of a common fear—disapproval. If you asked him why he worked so hard, he would tell you that he only wanted to be a good husband, father, and Christian. He tried to do what was expected of him and what he expected of himself. Having never enjoyed his father's attention, he had become a man who had never been a boy.

The boy's job for his first twelve years is to learn well to express his needs and have them met. He is to learn his feelings and how to express them so that they are understood. In doing these increasingly complex tasks, the boy learns what is truly satisfying and what is not.

The boy who is equipped in this way has learned what he likes from his mother's excellent attention and how to feed himself by his father's encouragement. He has become a part of his community and is recognized as such. This boy is ready to become a man. Yet, it seems that this is not the case for most twelve-year-old boys. Some may be close, but for many boys the path towards manhood is nothing like what we have described.

The dysfunctional family is one in which the adults try to be children, while the children try to be adults. This inversion of roles is the best way of describing the effects of trying to be an adult without first learning the lessons of being a child. As we have also pointed out, these lessons are cumulative. Man "stuff" builds on boy "stuff" rather than replacing boy "stuff."

ENTITLEMENT AND LEARNING WHAT YOU CAN PRODUCE

Entitlement. Perhaps the best way to describe the boy who has completed his training is to consider entitlement. The boy who has been weaned correctly knows how to ask for what he needs. He considers himself to be entitled to have those needs met just because he exists and simply by asking. The boy who then has been trained well by his father also knows what to ask for. He knows to ask for those things which satisfy and to avoid those lures and baited hooks that do not.

The sign of a complete boy is that he can ask for and receive what he needs with joy and without guilt or shame. While this will appear selfish to some, it is absolutely essential as a foundation for giving as an adult. The one who cannot receive freely cannot give freely.

Jesus, we are told, left his riches in heaven because he chose to. It is precisely because he knew he was under no obligation, guilt, or shame if he kept everything for himself that we can appreciate his gift. Entitlement precedes giving.

In the trial of Ananias and Sapphira, the first Christians to receive the death penalty from God, a pivotal point by the prosecution was entitlement. "While it was in your hand were you not free to do with it what you wanted?" asked the apostle Peter. He made it clear that giving was to be done freely. God, in fact, says that he does not want gifts given by compulsion, but he loves a cheerful giver. Only a man who has first been a boy can experience this truth. Perhaps this is part of why we cannot enter the kingdom of God unless we become as little children.

The problem for those who try to become men without first becoming boys is that they can only give if they are compelled to do so by shame or guilt or fear. This becomes a good test for any man who wonders whether he has completed the task of being a boy. If you consider keeping your time, money, energy, or other resources for yourself, do you feel guilt and shame? If so, you have not learned entitlement. Do you experience guilt, shame, or embarrassment if someone gives something to you? If so, then you have not learned entitlement. The result is a loss of joy. The boy receives with joy. His food brings joy. His affection brings joy. His time brings joy. To the boy, receiving is joy. So it is that Solomon concludes his analysis of a man's life in Ecclesiastes by saying that everything beyond receiving what we need is emptiness (Eccl 8:15). A man who looks for joy elsewhere will not find it.

Solomon also points out that the other source of satisfaction for a man is to enjoy his work. He is careful to point out that it is not the accomplishments that count. Accomplishments are also emptiness. It is simply the work of his hands, that which comes out of him that satisfies. So, to Solomon, the tasks of the boy are the center of life, to receive your food, be loved, and to enjoy what you do.

Learning what you can produce. The man who learns to receive without learning what he can produce is also in a very bad place. He has indeed mastered the job of the nursing child, but has not learned from his father to produce life. This man becomes an endless vacuum cleaner. Without guilt or shame, he will consume the world for himself. Not surprisingly, although his eyes "gleam through folds of fat," (Ps 73:7) as Solomon's dad would say, he appears to others like a giant tapeworm. He feeds freely on all he can possess, and yet he is still not satisfied.

Consuming is not a satisfying definition of a man. We must both take in and give out. The boy who has learned satisfaction from his father knows this well. He can see what satisfies and what does not. Consuming alone will never satisfy. The person who tries to reach satisfaction by consuming is doomed to consume more and more and more in the vain hope that more will satisfy. This is what powers many of the things we currently view as addictions, but it takes root deeply in a consumer society. We are to believe that satisfaction will come from the resources we consume. More expensive is better. More is better. Buy and be satisfied. You are what you eat, or wear, or drive.

Entitlement without production will not satisfy and is deadly as well. For this reason many people run away from entitlement. Some people fear that teaching their children that they are entitled to their needs and feelings will breed selfish children. Because such parents operate out of fear, they build guilt and shame in their children rather than entitlement. These children never complete the task of childhood and so can never become adults that will give and receive freely and joyfully. There will always be "strings attached."

Most of the current trends on psychotherapy and popular psychology address this problem of the child within. They are secular attempts to find the kingdom through becoming like a child. They are correct in so far as they go. We must all be children first. The men's movement also affirms this need to be boys. Men who have not been boys have no roots with which to nourish the rest of their tree. They have far less support for the growth of their fruit.

Christians, on the other hand, have had a tendency to teach sacrificial giving at the expense of entitlement. In Sunday school they begin to teach that it is better to give than to receive, not because it is a step of maturity and so it is more gratifying, but because it is more "righteous" to give than to receive. Guilt then falls on any who prefer to receive or even who feel entitled to receive. This is the road to disaster.

A friend of mine tells a story which could be repeated by many a Christian child. His father had given him a new bicycle for his tenth birthday. A few weeks later a neighbor lost his car and needed transportation to get to work. Acting on the principle that it was more blessed to give than to receive, this father gave the bicycle to the neighbor. My friend was expected to be happier about this arrangement than he had been to receive the bicycle to begin with. Although he was old enough to understand the neighbor's plight and wanted to help, he could not get past the loss of his bicycle. Try as he might, my friend was not happy, nor has he ever become happy, about his loss of a bicycle. He continues to give and give, he even lives out of his car at times to give his children a private school education, but he is still not satisfied. Always haunting him is the feeling that he has lost what is precious to him.

Now, don't get me wrong. It was not losing the bicycle that made him live in a car. These are only symptoms of a boy who never learned entitlement. Some days he can be one of the most dissatisfied "good Christians" you might ever meet. In fact, he is nearly a saint by some standards, but his joy is not always there. He became a man without ever having been a boy.

THREE MISTAKES WOUNDED MEN MAKE

The three classic mistakes of a man who has not learned to be a boy are to try to gain value or satisfaction by consuming, to seek value or satisfaction through action, and to proceed through life following some set of guidelines, goals, or rules without seeing if they bring him any satisfaction. Any boy could do better than these wounded men.

The Consumer. Bill was meticulous about his clothes. Bill shopped at the right stores and drove a BMW with a great stereo system. Never one to make a splash, Bill was understated but always had the right wine for the occasion, the house in the right neighborhood, and just the right friends. Although he was only "worth" $750,000, many of his friends were millionaires. Bill had winning ways when he wanted to.

Bill left his wife for a younger woman. He left his new job for one with more prestige and financial security that let him spend his days with the very wealthy. He moved into a new house with his new wife in a better neighborhood and had new kids. Some of his old friends were offended by this and began saying that Bill kept his brain behind his zipper. He left his old friends for better ones who didn't bring up his ex-wife or kids. Bill now throws bigger parties for more people, has replaced his old BMW with a new one, has a faster computer, manages a larger staff, and eats in finer restaurants.

Bill also traded in his doctor on a new one. It seems that some of the nurses in the doctor's office were becoming amused by Bill's endless stream of worries about his body and his health. His doctor could find nothing wrong that merited treatment, even though Bill's tennis game was declining a bit. He fastidiously moved to healthier and healthier foods.

Bill did eventually go to see a therapist. The doctor was a prominent professor and owned several counseling centers. As Bill commented, the doctor charged top fee. Bill didn't see the need to stay long. Bill was consumed with consuming. What he could not consume he stored for later consumption. Bill had reached the American dream, but few people I know respect him as a man. He seems to think his value comes from what he buys and possesses.

The Doer. Some men take their value from what they do. Sam said he would never retire. He loved construction. At six every morning, seven days a week he found himself at the pancake house with the other contractors swapping stories and subcontracts. His truck and his tools went everywhere he did. Sam worked until late afternoon most days and took pride in his work. He was known to get in fights with homeowners who wanted inferior materials just to save money. He lost a few friends that way.

Sam's wife had a life of her own and, truth be known, had told a few of her friends that Sam just watched TV and was unpleasant at home. So she didn't care that he was still working at age sixty-nine.

Sam took a vacation one time with a friend and set off to see the country, but they got in a fight before too many miles. His friend nearly left him in a café and let him find his own way home. Sam was not much for conversation unless he was reminiscing about what quality redwood used to be like.

When Sam had a heart attack and found he could not work, he became miserable. All he wanted to do was die and it took him very little time to let everyone know that. Soon his visitors began to feel that it wouldn't be such a bad idea, although perhaps they didn't really mean it in their hearts.

Sam was a contractor. It wasn't that he did construction, he had become a contractor. What he built was who he was. To see his finished work was to see him. No wonder he did not like inferior materials and would rather lose a friend. Aside from what he did, Sam was not able to recognize himself. Sam thought his value came from what he could put out. Those who trusted his work will miss him, especially if their next contractor does bad work.

The Rule-maker. Paul was as dutiful a pastor as any church board would ever hope to find. He was a man of experience, principle, commitment, and virtue. He did not lack compassion for his congregation and visited both the weak and strong. Paul was a man of vision and with his help churches grew. An excellent pastor, he taught and studied carefully, but not so carefully that he left no room for change or uncertainty.

If this wasn't enough, Paul was a family man. He loved his wife and three children. Paul even loved the family dog, although he might not admit that to everyone. One day Paul came to see me because he was just not sure whether to continue as a pastor. Something was wrong and he couldn't quite put his finger on what it was. Being a man of high principle, he needed to find out what was wrong, why his work seemed to be unfulfilling. Try as he might, Paul could simply not figure out what was the right thing to do.

Paul's father was a pastor. He had good parents. They cared for him and never abused him. To this day, they call and see each other often. His family had taught Paul all the right things. Paul knew how to evaluate, solve problems, and do what was right. In seminary Paul even improved on the things his family had taught him, but there was one thing Paul did not know. Paul had no idea what satisfied him. He did not even realize that he should know what satisfied him. Somehow, asking what satisfied him seemed "fleshly" and wrong, a bit too selfish.

Living without knowing what really satisfied him had almost burned out his candle. Paul had too many right choices every morning and no way to know which of them brought life to himself. A good pastor would return a phone call, drop in on a sick man, take his wife to lunch, meet with the board members over lunch, have lunch with a homeless man, stop in at his daughter's school to see her during lunch, take the dog for a run, take time away for quiet prayer, prepare carefully for Sunday's sermon, read up on the topic for the men's retreat, and then there were all the good things a pastor would do in the afternoon and evening.

Without knowing which of these things brought satisfaction, Paul could only continue to review his principles and set priorities, but it troubled him that so many good things *never* got done. In time he ran out of gas, began to dread his work, the phone calls, even meeting with his board. Perhaps, he reasoned, I am not meant to be a pastor, or I would have joy in my life.

This pastor knew that his value did not come from his work or from what he possessed. He ran out of gas, though, because as a human being he needed to be satisfied by his labor and food, but he had no hint on how to choose wisely. His father before him had not known what satisfied and never thought to teach his son. As a result, they would both go until they collapsed from exhaustion and wonder where the time had flown.

Satisfaction is the emotional fuel that keeps us running to meet the next challenge we face.

Between Bill who tries to be a man by consuming, Sam who is obsessed with his work, and Paul who has lost his way, we see a few of the pitfalls of trying to be a man without first becoming a boy. Many more stories of such men can be found in Gordon Dalbey's book *Father and Son: The Wound, the Healing, the Call to Manhood.*

Men have been trying to heal this wounded boy for some time. The "liberated man" who, in response to the women's movement, learned to feel and need, has learned one-third of the job of being a boy. If he thought this would please the women around him, he was wrong. For in learning to be sensitive, he has become a boy and then only what a mother would teach him about being a boy. Women want a man, not just a boy, and not a mama's boy. If he has also learned entitlement and to produce from himself, then he will have something to give and be in far less trouble, for now he knows two-thirds of what a boy should know. The final third of being a boy comes only from learning what truly satisifies. The boy who has learned all these things is ready to become a man. Although he will not live to satisfy women, he can become the man women seek.

Yuppie women, meanwhile, have been learning how to produce during the last two decades. They have learned two-thirds of being a girl; they can feel and they can do, though perhaps many of them have yet to learn what truly satisfies. Many are finding that they, too, have large defects in their ability to feel and are now taking care of their own inner child. These women are also dissatisfying to men who are not looking to find girls but women.

Trying to be a man without first being a boy is very discouraging. In the end, the imposter will be found out because he will consume too much or too little, work too much or too little, and never be satisfied. He will run out of strength just when he needs it, like the foolish virgins who ran out of light because they did not buy enough oil for their lamps.

Men who do not know how to be boys will fall asleep behind the wheel, because they didn't believe they needed sleep. They will believe the billboard that shows a glass of whiskey and the caption: "What a successful executive earns in a day." It will be a life of pain, as they fail to ask or ask amiss and so fail to receive. As pretenders to the throne, they demand in fear what they would freely be given in love, while they flee the power wielded by those entitled to possess and give.

Given this woundedness in the lives of so many men, we now need to explore what it means to become a man. There are just too many wounded little boys walking around in men's bodies wondering whether anyone will ever show them what it really means to be a man.

FIVE

Becoming a Man

THE MEN AT THE RETREAT gathered in small circles of eight to twelve guys, and the oldest man in the circle stood up. He went from man to man in the circle, placing his hands on their shoulders and proclaiming this simple blessing: "God, your Father, loves you and I declare this day in his name that you are a man. God is very pleased."

The men shake as tears well up in their eyes. They let the words sink in and speak haltingly in hushed tones. It is the same way at every retreat. Men of all ages hear for the first time that they are men, and God believes that is a good thing. Then the group surrounds the oldest man and repeats the same blessing on him. It is the burden of our generation of men to pass on what we did not receive. Inevitably, this simple ceremony is the high point of the retreats I lead.

Joel was a strong man with a firm handshake. He had a look about him that gave one the impression that Joel usually got his way. He sort of took over the couch as he sat down. Before long he informed us that he was a retired fighter pilot and father of three grown children.

"I want to become a man. I feel like a boy inside around men who are years my junior. That is why I came." Joel's words were clear, and he looked the other men in the eye.

Larry sat back in his chair with his legs sticking out like the ends of a wishbone. He told us that he was a federal marshal and the father of three children as well. "I'm always afraid," he said, "that I'll do something wrong and get yelled at. If anyone gets mad at me I feel like a little boy. I can't ever remember feeling like a man under pressure. I worry constantly."

Like many other men there, Larry and Joel were waiting for the time to come when they will feel like men inside. As they approach retirement, they experience a sense of loss and shame that what they thought would happen never did.

Steve told of his hope as a boy. "I thought that when I could walk out of the bathroom smelling of aftershave I'd feel like such a man!" But although we could still smell the Aqua Velva on him, he assured us it hadn't worked its magic.

"You should have used Old Spice," Joel smirked.

Others told how they had hoped that getting a wife, a career, or a promotion might make them feel like men, but it never panned out.

So, as the men gathered in the retreat center's conference halls, they turned to the older men waiting to hear the words that have never been said about them, "You are a man."

Joel went first. He was the oldest in his group. After he had blessed the others, they placed their hands on him. It was a sacred moment. Joel heard what every thirteen-year-old boy needs to receive from his dad and the men of his community. For Joel it had taken an extra forty years.

The blessing of manhood launches a boy on his next great adventure. It is an adventure with real consequences, real responsibilities, real costs, and real life. It is what real men are—alive.

Let us suppose for a moment that life is normal. We have a normal thirteen-year-old boy who knows what he feels and is able to express his feelings clearly. The boy knows what he needs and what will satisfy him. Although he is not perfect in these regards, he knows how to ask for the help he needs when he needs it. The boy knows that he has great value because God said so and therefore he is entitled to receive all the things he needs. In other words, this is a normal thirteen-year-old. Yet, the boy has observed that there is more to life than what he experiences. Men, it seems, have a power with each other that is out of range to him. He senses the pressure when men collide, and yet like the mountain rams, walk away unharmed. He is ready to discover a new meaning for a word he has known since pre-school—fairness.

"It's not fair," screams the child.

"We shall make it fair," says the man.

Manhood is all about fairness because for the first time the developing male becomes responsible to look out for his neighbor's needs in the same way he has regarded his own. "It's not fair" for the child means that his own needs and feelings were being ignored. "It's not fair" for the man could just as easily mean, "Your needs and feelings are not to be ignored."

The boy, who to this point has had his own needs to meet and his own satisfaction to seek, is about to meet his first major challenge. To be a man is to realize that his actions have an impact on others for whom he has responsibility. The man must work to see that others' needs are given the same consideration as his own. As the man's power increases, it is possible to take unfair advantage of weaker or less knowledgeable men, women, and children. A man will see to it that this inequity does not happen—first, because it will not be satisfying and, second, because it will mar his contribution to history. A man must love his neighbor as himself. Fair is fair.

A MAN IS A PART OF HISTORY

The step into manhood for the normal boy is found in this awesome discovery. He is a part of history. He is now ready to know that because he has lived, life will not be the same for other people. He will have his effect whether it be for good or ill. Understanding how he is to participate in history will be his challenge for the next decade or so. To start him out right, his father and the men of his village, those who know their history, will instruct him on how history works. Since the normal boy understands satisfaction, he immediately wants to know what sort of participation in history will be the most satisfying. By learning these secrets he will become a wise, good man.

Perhaps it is not right to call the means of participating in history "secrets," because they are so plainly seen. But to the untrained eye they appear as secrets, and the boy's eye is new at all this. By examining the history already passed, the boy can learn of the history yet to come. Still the thirteen-year-old is not skilled at seeing large patterns, so the history he must hear first is that of his own family and people, his own town and life. If he first understands what is nearby, he will soon grasp what is far away as well. These are the stories that make a man. They are the true stories of how he came to be, who he is, and how through him others will come to be who they are.

Boys learn to be men through stories, his-stories. A man knows that he is not the only part of history. He wants his interests and those of others to be fairly represented. When he is thirteen the new man starts thinking, "What is a fair bargain? How do I deal with others so that it meets their needs and my needs?" He thinks to himself, "What I do will have an effect on other people." That is how he does it.

REDEMPTIVE HISTORY

To the Christian, all history is redemptive. Redemption can be painful because the truth about us is often kind of ugly. The truth about men is that they can handle the pain of knowing the truth, so they must learn their story whether it hurts or not. Men learn to grieve when the story hurts, but it is not grieving that redeems the story, that can only be done by the eyes of heaven.

Being a part of history has some very important ramifications. All of a sudden what we do begins to matter. Who we are begins to matter a great deal. All of history is part of an ongoing fight, and we are participants whether we want to be or not. Here is one story that every new man must know. The story goes like this:

God created the world, and he said to the two people he put in charge, "I need you to know that while this is a wonderful garden, my creation has been infected by a very, very nasty virus. I am sworn to get rid of it. As I live, I will wipe it out. Only good will be eternal, evil will not survive. You need to know that anything that gets contaminated by that virus will get wiped out too. I am sworn to get rid of both the virus and its influence. So here is a word of advice: don't mess with that virus, because as soon as you do, you'll be on my list of things that have been infected and will not be eternal."

Of course, we humans, being the wise creatures that we are, made a mess of it. Now Adam had already had a lesson on how to relate to the Lord God. Remember how he said, "Excuse me, Lord God, I noticed when I was checking out the animals that there are two kinds of them. But there is only one kind of me. I liked petting the kitten, playing with the dog, riding the horse, hugging the koala, laughing with the otter, and talking to the parrot, but could I put in a requisition: do you have a form—for one like me? I'd like to have this corrected."

And God said, "You know what? You have a point. I like your idea, and I will do just that for you." And he did. Adam found a problem, took it to God, God said, "No problem, I like your idea, we'll work on it together," so they did and it was better than before. They all looked at it together and said, "What a good day this is. Praise the Lord! That is how I like it."

We can still do that. We have an idea and take it to the Lord to say, "Here is a problem, can you do something about it?" And God says, "What a good point you have! Yes, I do like working on history with you. What do you suggest we do about it?" And so we talk it over until we have a plan.

Back in the garden, however, someone pointed out another problem to Adam. "Say! You guys don't know the difference between good and evil. By the way, there is a

tree over there with the answers to all your problems."
And so the tree that was supposed to point to God
became a god, the first of many trees to do so as men
began to carve them up, until they finally used one to try
to kill God himself.

Well, Adam should have known better because he knew
how to be a part of history. He should have gone to the
Lord God and said, "Lord God, it has come to my attention that we have another problem here in the garden.
What can you do about our lack of knowing good and
evil?" And who knows what the Lord God would have
done? I would have never guessed the woman solution,
would you? Just take a nap, lose a rib, add a few features.... I would have loved to find out what the Lord
God would have done about the tree, wouldn't you?

But that wasn't the way it turned out. Adam had his
influence on history. We all got infected and scheduled for
elimination. That is still the truth today. God will not tol-
erate evil to be eternal. Don't carry it with you or leave it
in your life, or it is termination for you.

The biggest surprise was that God provided a decontamination process. It could not be done by anyone who
was contaminated, and it would cost us our bodies. But
not to worry, new bodies would be in order after final
decontamination. Now he might have given us new bodies anyway without decontamination, we don't know. Like
I said, who would have guessed the Eve thing? God said
he would take us from glory unto glory, which means that
he isn't just decontaminating but always making the good
even better. This is the history we are a part of creating.

This is an important story every man should know. The only
problem is that the snake would like us to forget about our part
in history or make us believe that we only can play a negative
role. That way we will not know that what we do is going to
make a difference in how history turns out. As soon as we for-

get, we go back to acting like little boys. Little boys are only concerned about themselves. What really generates problems is when these "little boys" inside men's bodies take control and start running homes, churches, and businesses for the purpose of avoiding any pain themselves.

The Bible has long stories about these "boys" who didn't know or care that they were forming history and set off instead to find pleasure and avoid pain. One such story takes up about as much space in the Book of Genesis as the first five days of creation. It goes on to take up the whole Book of Ruth and ends in 1 Samuel. What is the legacy of men who ignore their place in history?

Take Judah, the man the tribe was named after. His dad prophesied about him that the king would come from his tribe. Not only did that mean the little king that would rule the people, but the big King that would wipe out the virus. What an exciting part in history. Judah's oldest son might be the king or maybe his oldest son, only time would tell.

So what did Judah do? His oldest son died without leaving a child, but he did leave a wife. So to produce an heir Judah gave the wife to the next son, who also died without leaving a child. This left Judah only one son. He then forgot about the promise and decided that the girl was a jinx. This girl was too much bad luck for God to overcome, but the girl wanted son three to give her a child. Perhaps you remember the story of how she pretended to be a hooker and Judah got her pregnant. He showed that he was into avoiding pain and finding pleasure whenever and wherever he could. When he found out that his daughter-in-law was pregnant, he didn't want any pain for himself and decided to have her killed. When he found out that it was his child he said, "She is more righteous than I." That was the family line for the King.

But incest is not the way to conceive a king, and God said that no one could be king for ten generations after an illegitimate birth (Dt 23:2-3). And so it is that in the Book of Ruth, we hear the end of this story as the last few generations count down to Jesse at number nine and King David at ten. God kept his promise, but Judah slowed it down for ten generations. When Judah was wandering down the road thinking of fleeting sexual pleasure, he neglected to think of the effect on the next ten generations. Four hundred years is a long penalty for not acting like a man, a part of history.

OUR PLACE IN HISTORY

God stays involved with history in order to redeem it. He can do that two ways, by stamping out evil or by redeeming us and our history with us. For this reason we need not fear our pain, shame, or ugliness, for God can and will see us through to redemption. He can take the worst situation and, by redeeming it, find a place in redemptive history for us. Those who see these things done become the eyewitnesses of history. In this we find one of our greatest points of participation in history; we are God's witnesses and the bearers of hope that decontamination from the virus of sin is a reality.

Each man has the history of his own personal redemption which he can share with others. Redemption does not make bad things good. Bad is still bad, but the Lord God can look at the bad and say, "I could make something out of that." Let me give you an example of redemption at work in my life.

When I was twelve I began to take an interest in manly matters like girls and transportation. I had always kind of liked Margie, so I really wanted to impress her. It was the fashion for teenage boys in our neighborhood to give the girls rides on the handlebars of their bicycles. Now that I was twelve and had a new bicycle, I had a way to do it. Still, I had never tried it before, so I figured to play it safe by letting the girl sit on the back instead. Margie had never been asked before, so I rode right in front of her and said, "How about taking a ride on the back of my bicycle?"

She said, "I'm not sure my parents would let me do that." But she walked over to my side. I looked at her coolly.

"Don't worry, I am a good driver. Come on, Margie."

In moments we were headed down the driveway and around the corner. It was just then that things started to go wrong. Our trajectory was a new gravel driveway. Not an ordinary gravel driveway, this one was crushed rock. Since gravel was scarce, contractors took big rocks and crushed them down into little sharp pieces. The result was a pleasingly uniform, grey, crunchy surface.

As I went around the corner, fast enough to impress Margie, the bike flew out from under me. Down we went on fresh gravel. Wishing to be manly and not let Margie hit the ground, I bravely put my knee down to catch the bicycle. Margie didn't get a scratch but I had a knee full of gravel.

The rocks were deeply imbedded and the few I pulled out really stung. Thinking that there must be a better way, I limped over to a clinic right away. My knee hurt like crazy and I wanted something done about it. Being manly about it, I was careful not to cry.

At the clinic, some angels of mercy proceeded to grab tweezers and pull the stubborn rocks out. Then they took these wonderful little scissors (I don't know if you have ever seen them), which started off in one direction, and then took a sudden turn to the left. (For some reason medical people never have straight scissors for anything.)

Those little scissors did a great job cutting up my knee. I wouldn't have minded if they had given me a shot first, but they just cut away saying, "This stuff has got to come out of here." They snipped away and I turned pale. You know it felt terrible. When I winced and pulled away, the nurses growled, "Hold still!" They didn't need to say, "Take it like a man," because I already knew that part of my duty. A man would not be bothered by pain.

After they bandaged me up, I went home. For some reason my parents didn't notice what had happened. For one thing, I often limped because my weak ankle was constantly getting sprained. In addition, my parents were prone to a certain disregard for bodies anyway. So for whatever reason, even though my jeans were torn up and bloody, they never noticed I had injured my knee. Perhaps they were too busy with their missionary work, because if they had noticed they would certainly have taken action.

A couple weeks later I was walking around and I smelled this awful odor. I didn't know what it was, but it seemed to be coming from me, of all places. I pulled up my blue jeans and noticed that my bandage was all yellow, sticky, and nasty. It occurred to me that the highly objectionable odor might very well be coming from that source. That bandage looked like it should smell bad, so I pulled it down. Suddenly everything underneath the bandage boiled up white. Hundreds of little maggots swarmed everywhere.

I knew I had seen worms like that before when I had kicked over the carcass of a dead cat. The white swarm was everywhere under the dead body, and they moved amazingly fast. This, however, was not a dead cat, this was my leg. My first reaction veered towards losing my breakfast. My second was, "I'm dead!" I heard the words come right out of my mouth, "I'm dead! What am I going to do?"

Logic steadied me in a bit. Obviously I wasn't completely dead, but what was happening? The only answer was to go back to the clinic again. I was terrified. It is funny now, but I was terrified then. So to make a long story short, they found the scissors again and it was another awful moment. They didn't give me a shot that time either. Like a man I took it without crying.

That story went into my trauma history. And to tell you the truth it caused me to feel a little resentment towards my parents. How was I supposed to know when to change bandages? The nurse yelled at me about it, but I didn't know you were supposed to change bandages. They didn't tell me that before. How was I supposed to know about that? It seemed to me that my parents should have helped me out and noticed my plight. I felt like a neglected child. Thinking about maggots in my knee did not make me feel good about myself or about my parents.

Eventually I decided I had to work through these feelings. I had to express them to God and tell him the truth about what had happened and ask him to heal the experience and to redeem it. By this time I was in my early thirties. Who knows how God could redeem maggots? In time I even forgot about it.

One day a woman came in for therapy and said to me, "I don't know how to tell you this." After that she started getting more and more upset. Finally, she said, "When I was a child, my parents locked me in a coffin with some maggots. They said that if I didn't do what they wanted me to do, which I didn't want to do, that they were going to leave me in there and those maggots were going to eat me alive."

Then she said, "You don't know what it is like to have maggots in you!" Suddenly a very strong picture with a very intense odor came into my mind. I empathized at a very deep level with what it was like to have maggots in you, to be a child, and to be terrified and think maybe you are dead. She kept saying, "You don't what it is like to think maybe you are dead and they are going to eat you up."

"I do, I do understand." I said. You see, at that moment the Lord finished redeeming that maggot story. At that moment, I knew inside it was worth having maggots and worth forgiving my parents. It was worth it to say to this anguished woman, "I don't care if you had maggots in you or not, the Lord God still loves you and he thinks you're a wonderful person. He will not reject you for having maggots in you."

And she said, "Oh, but I'm not like you."

What a wonderful opening. It must have been the Spirit at work. She thought she knew God could love me because I never had maggots in me—but not her. We know better. That is redemption history. And I ask you, how could someone arrange those strange bits of history on their own? I dare say most people have not had maggots. But the Lord God knew enough to put two people together that needed to give comfort to each other. A special moment was arranged by God. I must praise God for that—it's part of my history now.

I tried to tell my parents this story, and they were mortified.

They could not get into the redemptive value of the story at all because they were just too busy feeling bad about themselves as parents. A long time back that would have given me some degree of satisfaction. Now I want them to rejoice with me. There are many things in our lives that work that way. God can use them all to his glory.

You see our stories are our histories, there is no changing them. They have made us what we are, and we must tell ourselves the truth. Redemption is our only hope if we do not like our stories. The first thing I have many men do when they arrive for counseling is write an autobiography starting before they were born. Then in turn we focus on preschool years, grade school, junior high, high school, college or career starts, marriage, and on into the present. We look for the "maggots" in their lives and prayerfully ask for redemption of their stories. We take equal care with the hurts each man has caused to others or himself, asking for their redemption as well. By sharing these redemptive stories with their friends, wives, and children, these men become at last a part of redemptive history. They know they are men with a story worth telling.

Yet even as men claim their own part in redemptive history, they need to be aware of three killer myths in modern society that threaten to enslave them. We tackle these next.

SIX

Three Killer Myths

I RON JOHN IS THE NEW ICON FOR MEN. Iron John is running hard to catch other icons like John Wayne and John Lennon were for two different generations of men. For Aluminum Bill, Magnesium-alloy Dean, and Tin Tom, *Iron John* is the Wild Man. He is an inspiration to the men's movement which has turned to ancient myth to find out who men really are.

Myths have been around for millennia, and I enjoy a good myth as much as the next guy, don't you? There is much to be learned from myths, even the mytho-poetic men's movement with its Jungian analysts and its emphasis on the wildman, the warrior, and the king. It offers much that will help us grieve for the lost father. Yet, not even the poets would say that myths make you a man. Myths only teach, and some teaching kills while other teaching brings life.

Some myths lie embedded in the fabric of society, lending strength or confusion to all who trust their hidden patterns. Occasionally these beliefs become connected to a personality or story and so become visible. Here are three killer myths whose patterns have shaped many men today.

MYTH ONE—MEN CAN'T HANDLE THE TRUTH

Somewhere in the mid-seventies writers began to take notice of men. I'm not sure they thought all that highly of us, but at least they had some compassion. They began to write about the "fragile male ego." That was wonderful for men and women because, for the first time in quite a while, men were allowed to have needs. The fragile-male-ego school said men have needs and feelings too. They are not the rocks they appear to be, living just to do heartless things. Inside they have needs and feelings just like women. It was really different than popular culture—liberating, some might say. Men were like women and not nearly as "macho" as the strong, silent type might suggest.

So it was that among compassionate, enlightened circles men were seen as having become hard and silent because they lacked the strength women received from talking. "Men can feel pain," was the basic message, "so don't beat them endlessly or they may break." It was soon apparent how quickly men retreated from the onslaught of feelings and words into silent or angry pain, so the myth of the fragile male ego was born. It was a myth or story to explain why men ran from feelings—especially women's feelings. As the men fled in droves, the myth grew to mean more than just "men have a breaking point" and came to mean "men can't take the truth."

While men fled, the sexual revolution gave them room for some liberated needs. Perhaps it was payback for the women, as if to say, "Hey! I can talk about something that makes you squirm too!" The need men claimed for their own is found in the phrase, "Men have certain needs," which most people understand as a reference to sex.

To this day many men think sex is all they really need. Well, there is one exception to that: men might need a drink. Men certainly say that. (Of course, the drink must be alcoholic; no man would need water.) So men need sex and drinks, and the luckiest dog is the man who finds a woman who will give him both.

All of this has grown up in the midst of a culture that denies that men have emotional needs. Men aren't even allowed to need sleep. They have had to create euphemisms to talk about sleep. "I've got to hit the sack," or "catch a little shut eye," anything but say, "I need sleep. I'm tired." Real men don't admit needing sleep, let alone anything else. Other needs just don't fit in. Little wonder that many men do not operate well.

But the fragile male ego finally made room for a man to have needs and feelings, even if he didn't acknowledge what they were. Women, in particular, were taught to understand these men who did not know how to say, "I need to go to sleep." They were to understand that when men growled and harumphed, they really meant "I'm tired." A wife needed to understand that if she said to her hubby, "You mean you need to go to sleep?" she might hurt his feelings of masculinity, so it was better to let him wander off to bed with the understanding that tomorrow he would be all right.

Well, I love the compassion this produced. I'm all for anything that will send a little love our way (not that we need it, you understand), but a little snake in the grass came along with the fragile-male-ego myth. The problem was that the truth had to go. What came along with the fragile male ego was a fear of telling men the truth about themselves. You can't tell men the truth if you are hurting their feelings because they have a fragile male ego. You can't tell them if they are messing up their family or being irresponsible at work. The only people who can handle the truth are the kids and the women. The family will cover for Dad and say, "Oh, yes, he has a drinking problem. Yes, he is creating problems at work." They can understand the truth, but don't tell a man the truth because he can't handle it, his ego might break.

Even in the area that men had kept for themselves, the myth grew. As women began to talk about orgasms, men began to feel that these, too, were somehow a reflection on the man. Faking a climax seemed better than the truth at times as women believed a man might be devastated and emasculated to discover that his most intimate relationship was less than ideal.

When we can't tell the truth, we can't be a part of real life. We can't know our part in history. We can't even begin to measure our impact. We can't know who we are and what we do if we don't start with the truth. As a result, there are a lot of men who are very confused about how much power they really have. They don't know how much they can handle. They particularly don't know if they can handle pain or not, so they simply "stuff" it.

MYTH TWO—MEN SHOULDN'T SHOW PAIN

There is a fairly good chance that the strong, silent type of man who may have inspired that compassionate, fragile male ego myth believed that men shouldn't show pain. I think that long ago this grew out of the knowledge that men could handle pain. Men had the strength to experience pain, but rather than face the grief of World War I and World War II, Korea, Vietnam, genocide, oppression, and lost fathers, showing no pain became a way to show off. It became a way to test other men, to become more of a man than others, and even to become a man. Gangs, tribal initiations, boot camp, high school football, "cold war spies," and tough guys of all stripes relied on this test of manhood. I was very much taken as a boy by the story of the young stoic warrior that let his pet fox eat him to death without flinching or crying and so became a hero of ancient Sparta. Consequently, it made sense to let nurses cut me with their scissors without showing pain because, as any twelve-year-old boy would, I wanted to be a man.

Well, the snake was back in the grass again. Instead of learning that men can survive pain and need not fear it, men began to think that pain was manly, so they decided not to avoid it. Others made the assumption that men who did not show pain must not feel pain. Sons of the former men avoided pain in order to avoid the stupidity of their fathers, while the sons of the latter men avoided pain because it felt painful to them and they feared it made them less than men.

Men who do not speak honestly about pain will never know how much they can take. What started as strength ended as deception. A man might know that he can handle physical pain, especially if it is inflicted on a football field. But can he handle the pain of feeling sad, sad, sad—so sad that it would make him cry? Can he handle that? He doesn't know.

What did our fathers teach us about how to handle emotional pain? Did we see them facing it, going through it, and teaching us, "You know, son, this will hurt, but we can take it"? Only rarely, I think. Usually, they were simply silent and detached about it, or stupidly suffered unnecessary pain without ever telling us. In fact, truth itself is often painful, so silence often greets the truth and men retreat to the shelter of the fragile male ego or the suffering, silent stone.

Yet all of us know the moment will come when we must face the truth about ourselves, and we say, "This is going to hurt." If we really look at ourselves, there is a good chance we are going to be ugly. How painful to be ugly. To be honest, what man can't say, "I've done something ugly," or, "There is something wrong with me. If I look at how I grew up, there is going to be something ugly there too. And then what? What will I do with that pain? Will it destroy me? Will it alter me so that I won't ever be able to be a man? Will I show pain in front of other guys? Will I still be a man if I feel emotional pain?"

An alternate strategy for men is to avoid feeling pain entirely if possible. To do so requires that all pain be borne by someone else. This is perhaps a good definition of evil, for that is the result of letting others bear our share of pain. These men will try to take control, because if they are the ones in control they don't have to feel pain. See how wonderfully that works!

I saw this illustrated in the store recently. A four-year-old boy acted up so his father hit him and then hit him again, saying, "Shut up, or I'm going to give you something to really cry about!" The boy had embarrassed his dad by making a scene, and this dad knew he was going to get control of that situation. No one was going to see that he didn't know how to control his kid. It was a power struggle right to the end over who would be in control. The dad was not going to be embarrassed and feel any emotional pain. If anybody was going to be feeling some pain, he knew exactly who that was going to be. It didn't matter how much power it took, he would use all he needed to be in control and avoid the pain. Even though the only pain for the father was embarrassment, he was not going to take it.

MYTH THREE—A MAN SHOULD ALWAYS BE IN CONTROL

Being in control is perhaps the main method used by people to avoid having to feel pain of any kind. The person in control can ostensibly make events turn out in ways that avoid discomfort to themselves.

What are the best ways to be in control? Two of the favorites are using threats and blaming people.

Threats. Threats are a good way to get control of a situation. Do you know that Jesus never threatened anyone? We are told that in 1 Peter 2:22. Many people tell me that they can't raise kids without threatening them. Others say you can't run a business without threats. You need to intimidate people from time to time. Perhaps Jesus failed to grasp this point.

What would life be like if men didn't threaten? The fact is people can't be controlled. God gave children and adults free will. He doesn't rescind the free will just because we aren't behaving. Anytime we try to control something that can't be controlled, it will make us feel out of control. The paradox is that a man who tries controlling others will soon feel out of control himself. It will drive him crazy.

A man can't control his girlfriend, wife, children, employees, or anyone else. He may hope to influence them in a positive manner, but he can't control them. Not even God will control them. God had two children. He put them in a garden and they blew it. God could have done better if he was in control all the time.

I could never do as poorly as Jesus did. I couldn't stand it. He worked with twelve guys intensively for three years. One of the twelve was a suicide. If I had a one-out-of-twelve ratio, I'd quit as a therapist. Not only that, Peter—the leader of the bunch—failed Jesus just when he needed him most. I couldn't stand to have as poor a success-to-failure ratio after three years of intensive work as Jesus did. I don't think I could take the pain of watching the disciples grow and then fail—again and again. How much pain can a man take? Jesus experienced extreme pain and yet he did not threaten or blame.

Blame. To the best of my knowledge, God has never been interested in blame. Blame is deciding whose fault it is. When things went wrong in the Garden of Eden, God did not ask whose fault it was. He only wanted to know, "What happened here?" God is interested in truth. Others have said: it was her fault; it was his fault; it was the snake's fault; it was God's fault. We need to make a clear distinction between descriptive truth and blame. For instance, when God interviewed the pair in the garden, his question was descriptive, "What happened here?" The man's answer was blaming or accusatory, "It is her fault."

Adam's ego was not too fragile for God to ferret out the truth. What did happen there? That is the question God wants every man to ask about his own life. Men who ignore this end up in the category that the Bible calls fools. In Proverbs, you will read a lot about fools. Fools are those who try to avoid pain and control other people.

The signs of a fool are: they are always right; they slander (blame) their family; they try to have everything their way so that nothing bothers or hurts them.

This was not Jesus' way. Did you ever stop to think about the Last Supper? Our Lord knew that in twelve hours they would be inflicting the most gruesome tortures upon him, and what was he doing? He was walking around talking kindly to people. Washing their feet, and even serving them a meal! He wasn't running away from suffering, was he? That is the strength that we are promised as men.

I don't think it ever works to run away. Even if we have never survived pain before, or had the courage to really face pain in our life, we can find the strength if we turn to God. To this day I don't know how Jesus did it. It is phenomenal. I would just be a basket case. I would not have a coherent thought if I was facing such gruesome torture and abandonment by my friends. Think of what a simple IRS audit would do to your concentration on a meal with your family. That is nothing compared to this.

This is the strength of a man. Strength we are promised if we are willing to face the truth. For that we have to be honest about ourselves, which leads us back to becoming a part of history. It is only when we are honest about ourselves that we can begin to know our place in history. That is what it means to be a man. A man is someone who becomes a part of history.

The role of blame in the men's movement. Before we can leave the subject of blame it is necessary to say something about the role of blame in the men's movement. To understand the men's movement, it is necessary to think clearly about blame. The main criticism of the men's movement comes from those who believe it to be another humanistic way of avoiding responsibility for one's troubles by blaming one's father. In this respect, the emphasis on the "father wound" described in the secular and Christian literature is seen as blaming the father for the son's problems. While it is not without reason to assume that some people will use any explanation as an opportunity to blame someone, this criticism of the men's movement tells us as much about the critics as about the movement.

In describing what is wrong with men, it is impossible to avoid mention of their fathers. Indeed, to avoid mention of the father would be to conclude that the father had no effect on his children, hardly a reasonable conclusion. As the men's movement has highlighted the important role of the father and given him honor, they have also pointed out his effects, whether for good or ill. To those who view explanations as blame, this becomes blaming your father for your trouble. To those who understand explanations as descriptions of history, blame is not the issue.

I have yet to find any writings in the men's movement that claim that fathers intentionally and knowingly produced the "father wound." The prevailing view of fathers is that they have no idea what value they have to their sons and are uncertain how to pass on much of what they do understand and value. Men hide the pain of sons who never knew how to be men.

What some call blame, others call truth. The truth of men's pain is difficult to ascertain because, as we have said, there are myths about men and pain which we must deal with first, myths that obscure the truth. The bottom line is that men do not tell the truth about pain! Swayed by myths, many men lie about pain. Men do not want to know the truth about pain. Men may not even know the truth about pain.

The absolutely screwy things men do to hide their pain would fill many books. Often it is so obvious to everyone else that the very effort seems pathetic. But when whole nations of men conspire together to deny their pain, the cover-up is far more convincing. Consider the following:

> It doesn't hurt when Dad is away.
> It doesn't hurt to have sex with many women.
> It doesn't hurt to be self-sufficient.
> I'm fine without friends.
> I don't really care for babies.
> I like intimidating people a little.
> I thrive on competition.
> I'm just not that affectionate.
> I don't feel like talking.
> I'm just a wanderer.
> I'm not ready to make a commitment.
> Sorry! I just keep falling asleep.
> It's just my temper.

Men will never begin to make sense of life until they admit that the games they play are ways to avoid the pain they claim they don't feel. Too many men do not tell the truth about pain, which is too bad. Perhaps if more men knew they were men, they might see the value in suffering a bit.

With these distorted views of what it means to be a man, what's a father to do? How can he help his son become a man? We discuss one possible approach in the next chapter.

SEVEN

How Sons Become Men

D AN STRUBLE THREW ANOTHER LOG on the fire. It was a "dad" kind of an evening with his baby daughter just starting to crawl around, one with plenty of interruptions. He and I had finished a discussion on weaning and gotten something to drink from the kitchen. Amanda was too young to benefit from our subject as she eyed me carefully. Dan turned and warmed up to his topic for the remainder of the evening.

"We just called out the third boy at church," he said, after reminding me of the ritual described in great detail by Gordon Dalbey in his book *Healing the Masculine Soul.* "Pastor Steve's younger son Adam just turned thirteen. Steve asked him to choose seven men in the church whom he respected to teach him how to be a man. I was one of the men he chose.

"On the appointed day the six other men showed up at Adam's house and called him out. They took him out to dinner together to celebrate his becoming a man. I was part of the calling out and dinner for the first two boys, but this time I was on Navy duty and returned just in time to prepare my house for the ceremony.

"After dinner, they brought him over to my home where we took turns telling him what he needed to know to be a man. We divided up seven topics and prepared well in advance what we wanted to say. We talked about peer pressure, drugs and alcohol, sexual purity before marriage, pursuing God's will, the importance of God's will, how to date and treat a woman, and man as warrior. I'm really excited about this."

Dan recounted how after the group had prayed for Adam, he had used his naval officer's sword to illustrate the parallels between forming a sword and making a man of character, discipline, and integrity. Everyone was delighted, particularly Adam, who then held the sword through each of the other presentations. The presentations were fast-moving when the men were well prepared and rambled when they weren't. All the men, however, had taken their role seriously. A tape of the presentations was given to Adam and the evening ended, but not the impact on the men or the boy. Each one knew he was a part of the community of men and a part of history.

Perhaps it will not surprise you to hear that many men have no idea when or how they came to be men. The three boys that Dan has helped to become men will probably have no such problem. Of course, just as it took them twelve years to become boys, it will take these young men many years to become men in the fullest sense.

When, after more than four thousand hours of practice, I was granted my license as a psychologist, I still felt very shaky about being on my own. I was a psychologist, but I knew there was much I still had to learn. In the same way, a thirteen-year-old boy becomes a man but knows that most of what it means to be a man is yet to be learned.

The boy who passes thirteen without recognition begins to feel the internal tension of being a man without a rite of passage and an idea of how to proceed. He is left on his own and to the mercy of his peers to invent a way to be recognized as a man. In fact, men often take very circuitous routes to prove they are really men. When I took scuba diving lessons, I had a chance to see how men aboard dive boats proved to themselves that they were now really men.

On board dive boats, there was a simple and often repeated ritual among men who were meeting for the first time. This simple test of masculinity required only three comments—two about women and one about men. Upon meeting the men would talk briefly about diving. Then the man who had first approached the other would make a crude sexual remark about women and how much he liked them. Typically, he would follow that up with a gay-bashing comment and conclude with another demeaning sexual remark about women. Now that their manliness had been established, the men could talk more about diving, be friendly with each other, and ask one another about equipment. Just about every man on the boat seemed to follow this formula. It made me wonder how I might make it as a man if I wanted to dive since I can't stomach insults to homosexuals or crude comments about women. It has also helped me appreciate more the alternatives we can provide among the community of men in the church.

Gordon Dalbey suggests in *Father and Son* that a great struggle to separate a boy from his mother and unite him with the community of men is what ushers a boy into manhood. Dalbey sees the rite of passage as separating the boy from the woman in the form of his mother. Other writers in the men's movement, such as Robert Bly and Sam Keen, concur.

But I see this rite as simply a passage from boyhood into manhood. It is, in fact, the first conscious identity shift that a male will experience. Unlike his weaning, this time he goes into the crucible of change with his eyes open, but not knowing who he will become. Strengthened by the community of men and the confidence of both his parents, the boy undertakes the scariest of all journeys. He leaves the security of his known sense of self as a boy for a new, unknown identity as a man. Once a boy has made this journey, there will be no overwhelming fear as God calls him to new identities later in life. For once you have made the journey from one identity to a greater one, you realize that you can survive the passage into the unknown.

God transforms us "from glory to glory" in a series of identity changes throughout our lifetime unless fear stops us from changing. Each time, we leave behind the comfort and restriction of knowing who we are for the greater glory of becoming someone we do not yet understand. Those who have experienced a rite of passage from boyhood to manhood will understand God's excitement at taking us on a journey, even though we do not ever know the outcome in advance.

It might not be apparent at first, but the passage into young manhood is the first real preparation for death—first, for the father; and, then, for the son. In death all one knows ceases to exist and a transformation takes place. We assume a new identity in a brand-new kind of existence. In facing this first major step, the boy makes the transition to another identity among the company of men and his family. He learns that a man can survive and face the unknown challenges he must one day confront alone at death. And yet he is not alone, for he is surrounded by a "great crowd of witnesses." In animist societies, the spirits of the ancestors fill the role that the witnessing spirits do for many a Christian martyr. No mere mortal can understand who we become when our bodies are motionless and cold, but we do know that we can survive radical changes in our "selves" and live. The rite of passage reduces our eventual fear of death. We have survived one passage and can survive others. We move from glory to glory.

As cited above, while many authors in the men's movement believe that the great struggle for a boy is to be separated from his mother and the society of women in general, I believe that a boy who had his father's involvement at weaning will not have an identity dominated by his mother. Therefore, there should be no further need for the son to separate from the mother. In his great leap to become someone more glorious than a boy, he will naturally want the support of both parents and the wider community. It seems to me that a boy who was raised by his father to express what is inside himself and seek satisfaction in his efforts will not be in for such a great struggle. Perhaps the normal transition into manhood would look something like the following pattern.

HOW A BOY BECOMES A MAN

A time of preparation. The preparations for manhood begin long before the boy turns thirteen. Each boy has already been through two passages; the first was done for him entirely by his mother. He has been told of this great day and each year it has been celebrated. This, he has come to know, was the first of many passages. His second passage required his help as he joined his father at the feast of his weaning and put food into his own mouth. These two passages, achieved and frequently reviewed, foreshadow still greater changes ahead.

Previews of coming attractions appear along the way to let the boy see how men behave. Some boys watch their fathers at home or go with them for trips to the store, for example. Other boys see men on television, visit Grandpa, or watch men at church, parks, and family gatherings. Just as importantly, the boy knows that he will become a man at the appointed time, so he does not have to interrupt childhood by trying to prove he is a man when he isn't.

Time away with Dad. The trip with Dad to learn how to be a man is the first concrete step in a boy's developing manhood. By going on a weekend together before the boy enters junior high school, the father is able to prepare his son for the changes ahead. Each boy needs to know that he will be growing in power—personal, sexual, intellectual, emotional, financial, social, and spiritual power. How he uses this power will determine what part he will play in history. Both he and his view of the world are getting bigger. Parents that don't prepare their children will later appear to be stupid in the eyes of their youngsters. This is an impressionable time for boys, a time when they really want closeness with their fathers and will readily listen to what they have to say.

I have devoted an entire book to this trip entitled *Rite of Passage: How to Teach Your Son about Sex and Manhood.*[1] On this trip a father has a chance to pass on the very best of himself to his son. It is surprisingly simple but profoundly moving. One friend of mine described the trip with his son as a sacred moment. "The only thing I can compare it to was my honeymoon," he said.

A rite of passage. The initiation or rite of passage means a change of identity, for the boy is no longer a child but now a man. Although it is frightening to leave behind one's identity in search of another, yet, in the company of those who have made the journey already and those who are making it with him, there is comfort and support. Thirteen is a great year. It was this initiation that Dan Struble performed, according to the model developed by Gordon Dalbey.

Mother's pride, encouragement, and natural concerns help the newly initiated youth experience that being a man is a good thing for women and help him keep the boy alive as the man grows. Without this balance, new growth might crowd out the old, leaving the man to wither. Just because you are a man doesn't mean you don't need your oatmeal!

A time of formation. The training in manliness starts in earnest as the young man receives his first roles in the community of men. Even though he practiced arguing over baseball rules in grade school, his first roles as a man are unglamorous opportunities to assist and observe men negotiating and working out problems to everyone's advantage.

Older men will frequently ask the question of two young men, "What will satisfy you both?" and expect the young men to work out such arrangements with each other. By modeling and encouragement, they will teach the fledgling men to take pride in bargaining strenuously for fairness. Because the older men pay attention to the beginners' progress, they will be able to help them see the needs of others and avoid abuses of power.

The roles available for young men often spring from the normal activities of life. Something as basic as hospitality and making sure that everyone is fed and able to participate in activities is a simple start. Young men who are looking for jobs learn fairness by negotiating the payment for mowing a lawn, painting a garage, or taking pictures for the neighbors' fiftieth anniversary.

More importantly, however, are the opportunities supplied by older men. Asking a young man's opinion and participation in discussions and decisions is very valuable training. Very often the men of the church will plan to help someone who is sick, invalid, abandoned, or impoverished. Younger men can be actively involved in taking inventory of needs, planning what needs to be done, or even taking charge of parts of the project that fit their skills, like making sure that all the watering and weeding is done in an invalid's yard. Young men are not cheap labor; they need to be a part of decisions such as who the men will choose to help this week and why.

In the family this can be accomplished by asking the young man to help plan his portion of the family budget, and who to include on family trips, vacations, holidays, and other activities. Planning activities that reach out to neighborhood children who lack stable homes or the lonely and elderly can help the young man balance his own needs with those of people who do not have the resources he has.

Sometimes a young man can be selected for a special task in order to help train him. Greg was picked by his father to choose the right site and boat rental for the men's fishing trip his dad was scheduled to lead. He helped Greg list the different features and advantages he needed so he could compare boats. Then he let his son call, negotiate, and finally select the best boat and site for the trip. It took quite a bit of time, more time than it would have taken his dad, but the training and sense of accomplishment that Greg experienced when he headed out with the men made it worthwhile.

Winging it. Solo flight arrives within five years of becoming a man. The independence and confidence developed among the community of men and from one's own family soon require decisions and consequences to rest on the young man's shoulders. The next step may be finding a job. It may mean moving into an apartment or going away to college. Solo flight usually involves making decisions like buying a car and other financial considerations such as deciding when to spend, save, or borrow money. Solo flight is never accomplished completely alone. In fact, deciding where you will work or who you will rent with are part of the risks in taking responsibility for your own life. The soloist must decide when to ask for help and advice and what mistakes or losses are tolerable.

Simon was a junior in advanced placement classes when he decided to exercise the option of skipping his senior year and enter college early. He had many ideas of what to do with his life, which in one way means that he had no idea what to do. Simon had started taking evening classes in junior college in order to learn Japanese. Instead of a graduation present, he asked his parents to send him on a trip to Japan. After careful consideration as a family, it was decided that he and two friends would take a seven-week trip through Japan. It was somewhat of a sacrifice on the part of his parents to send him there, but more importantly they wanted him to see what it was like in other cultures.

To make the trip work out, Simon had to plan it with the help of many people. Friends of the family and other parents helped Simon figure out transportation, lodging, food, and other needs for each day of the trip. When he actually arrived, he discovered that traveling in Japan, living in Japanese homes, and experiencing minority status left him constantly in need of negotiating what was good for him, his traveling companions, his hosts, and the friends he made.

When he returned home and started college, Simon was a changed man. His appreciation for his family, friends, and the help of others was greatly increased. Simon sought counsel from older men about career choices, changes in majors, and schools. He looked out for the needs of his friends and room-mates as well as his own. Unlike many other college students, he loved to call home and tell his parents what he was doing and received both their advice and admiration. In addition, he continued to discover what was satisfying for him and what was not. From calculus to aquariums, bicycles to sushi, sleeping with the window open to helping people escape cults, Simon examined it all. He was winging it.

But whether the soloist succeeds completely or not, his results are part of the family history to be applauded, analyzed, and in time refined for future flights. The young man expresses his feelings and explores his needs in discussions about what satisfied him and what didn't. Thus, he begins to understand the impact and benefits of his achievement for himself and others.

Fatherhood is on the horizon.

EIGHT

Life-Giving Manly Roles

"Men exist to fight wars and open the lids on jars."
Ralph M.

"I used to think I needed a man to get things off the top shelf, but now I have a stepladder." **Elsie B.**

A LOT OF GOOD TREES HAVE GIVEN their lives providing paper in the fight to say what a man really is. Television shows and magazine articles have provided all kinds of different images of manliness, most of them unappealing to the average man. Is it manly to be crude, stupid, inept, violent, lecherous, or power-crazed?

Most of these portrayals do not start with the premise that men should first be boys and then pass from that identity to the next as men. With so many straw men who have even failed to be boys trying to portray manhood, it is little wonder that unsatisfying pictures of men are the result. Yet being a man is a good thing which makes these kinds of crude portrayals all the more tragic.

For the first eight years that I was a counselor, I saw mostly women. Most of them came in to tell me how rotten men were. Fortunately counselors aren't considered people by their clients, and it took most women about a year to figure out that I was there at all. They would talk for a long time about how bad men were and how they hated men, then they would notice I was there one day and say, "But not you, of course." Eventually I tried to hide my masculinity because I didn't really want to let it be known I was one of them.

When dealing with disgruntled women, instead of being a man I was a "therapist," whatever that is. At some level I was ashamed of what men had done to them. I didn't want to be seen as a representative of all that hurtful and evil behavior.

After listening to horror stories about men and watching how the men on the dive boat behaved, I began to think that maybe there wasn't much good about being a man, after all. As the truth of what evil men have done continued to collect around me, my secret shame of being one of them grew.

It hasn't been popular to be a man for rather a long time, although the men's movement has begun to turn that around. In fact, being a man, and in particular a father, has been considered such a worthless thing that I never received a class on the subject in any of my four years of college or six years of graduate school. I don't mean that I didn't have a course on the subject. I mean that I never even had one class lecture devoted to the subject! That is how worthless the topic was considered to be. It is sort of shocking. Perhaps it is this disregard and hostility that has led to the men's movement in the 1990s.

At one point in the women's movement, men were considered drones by some radical feminists. I remember a group of women in college celebrating advances in biology that might eventually eliminate the need for men entirely. In theory not even donated sperm would be needed. With a new approach to in-vitro fertilization and a bit of screening, they envisioned a world free of the opposite sex. Eliminating men was proposed as a way to stop wars and clean up the planet. Now there is something to look forward to if, like me, you are male!

Two factors changed my secret shame of being a man, and before I knew it my counseling caseload changed from almost all women to mostly men. Both factors showed me the same miraculous truth: men have something good to offer. The first of these revelations came from the community of men and the second from a special group of women.

The first factor was seeing my name on a who's who list of fathering advocates in America. I guess writing a book on the subject is all that is needed to become a who. Now the truth is, I was not that impressed with myself as a father, but when Ken Canfield of the National Center for Fathering spoke of the fathering guilt that even good fathers carry, it occurred to me that being a father was indeed good. In fact, I had been and was good for my sons, as well as other men who have experienced a father deficit.

The second gift that changed my secret shame for being a man came from women. Not long after I became a who, several women read my book and told me that they would have liked to have me as their father. These women were incest survivors, some of them the very ones who had been so vitriolic about men earlier. The truth slowly sunk in. Being a man was good. Men were to be a source of good and life, protectors of what is good. There is no shame in that! It is not something that men do from time to time, but the essence of what they are created to become.

I did nothing to spread this good news, yet somehow men began to seek me out, asking to be taught the secret. There was little to it, and for the first time in my life I was really glad to be a man. It is important to see this does not mean I was really happy that I wasn't a woman. That had nothing to do with it. I couldn't do a thing about that, I simply happened to be male and being what one *is* is good—splendid, even. Whether others knew it or not, I represented good news to them because good news is what I was created to be, just as everyone else has been.

With this new appreciation for myself, I began to develop my own flair for life. Perhaps this is as good a place as any to say that as men become men, their wobbly efforts should soon begin to demonstrate a sense of style. Without this enjoyment of self-expression, men become merely functionaries, doers, and conveniences for others, as the quotes at the beginning of the chapter indicate. Yes, Ralph, men protect and serve, but they are also lovers. Lovers have a style to please the senses of their beloved. Yes, Elsie, men have bodies, bodies that sustain their needs. But they are also servants and the servant attends to details and the manner in which he serves. He does not simply perform service, but service flows from him expressed in his own unique style for the enjoyment of those served as well as himself.

Particularly in our consumer society, it is important to know that men have something to offer. A young man who possesses this knowledge will view all his actions and relationships differently. He knows himself to be a brother, friend, warrior, lover, servant, and even a source of life. All of these roles come to be expressed with a style that is uniquely his own. Whether he pursues marriage, schooling, or work, the contented, satisfied man is the one who knows that owning and consuming do not make him a man. It is not having pretty women and fast cars but giving and receiving life that bring joy. In the many roles of his life, a man can experience the goodness of being male.

MAN AS BROTHER

The identity of a man as a brother is one that carries over from childhood. Boys learn to be brothers. Then as men they learn to expand this type of relationship beyond the biological family. This is to say that men have brother-and-sister relationships with an expanding number of people. This component of a man's identity contributes greatly to his sense of fairness. A brother learns, long before he becomes a man, that the needs and feelings of his siblings matter. His entire family will have taken pains to point this out. Yet with siblings there is often a note of competition, or perhaps even the feeling that there isn't enough to go around. This must be corrected in the man. Each man must know in his heart that there is enough goodness for everyone so that he will always pursue the common good.

Dating is one extension of the brother role into the female world. In the great love poem, the Song of Solomon, the king refers to his beloved as his sister, "You have stolen my heart, my sister, my bride" (4:9). Perhaps this is not the average red-blooded American boy's dream, but then I can't say I'm too impressed with the average romance and marriage in our day. We would do far better to approach our dates as sisters than as mere entertainment for our viewing pleasure.

When I was dating, I noticed that most of the girls I dated were mad at the boy they had dated before me. Not uncommonly he had taken some liberties with her feelings or body that left her hurting. Knowing that someday I would be marrying one of these girls caused me to wonder what shape I would like my bride to be in when I received her. The maxim, "Do unto others as you would have them do unto you," took on some practical meaning. My dating goal, which I also taught to my sons, became dating in such a way that were I ever to meet the husband of a girl I had dated, he would want to shake my hand and thank me.

Even the word dating gives the impression of making an impact on history on a given date in time. A further spiritual truth was suggested to me by the view that we are the bride of Christ and consequently my treatment of all believers will fall in this category when I meet the "Groom."

MAN AS FRIEND

Like being a brother, friend is another role that boys carry over into manhood. Like brotherhood, friendship develops with age. The man has more depth to bring to friendship. It is a relationship for all seasons. Friendship for children provides a crucial source of comparison with others that is necessary for identity to form correctly. Children spend considerable effort comparing everything about themselves with others. While such comparisons can be used destructively, their healthy use is necessary for proper development. Friends are the yardsticks against which we measure ourselves. People tend to find yardsticks about their own size to measure themselves.

Friendships also help children learn to appreciate people who are different from themselves. Men need friends for both stretching and measuring. Men need friends for fun. Friends are the greatest help in developing a personal style, for they help us know how to express the things that make us uniquely ourselves and point out when that uniqueness is offensive. A man will often develop a style that complements his friends' styles. That can be good or bad, but the man without friends is usually an offense to eyes, ears, and nose.

It's worth noting, however, that men typically have a problem developing deep and lasting friendships, particularly with fellow men. The lack of close friendships among men has been attributed to many factors. Perhaps the most frequently mentioned reason is homophobia. This theory has gained some recognition among intellectuals but continues to receive the disregard it deserves from men at large. I believe that for most men their avoidance of close relationships with other males really stems from an unspoken fear of rejection by the male subculture, which is characterized by insulting and slightly hostile repartee. In common parlance, men refer to it as "just kidding around," under the cover of harmless banter about such things as sports, sex, fast cars, and the news. The hostility and insults usually come in the form of "put-downs" of newcomers and anyone who is different.

The truth is this kind of "just kidding around" can be downright deadly, especially in terms of its cumulative effect on men who are "put down." As compared to the more isolated trauma of actual seductions and assaults by other men, this subculture creates an emotionally charged climate that is experienced by nearly all men. The result is that even men who really do fear their homosexual feelings typically possess an even greater fear of rejection by their peers in this subculture.

As interesting and even plausible as the homophobia hypothesis sounds, a much simpler and compelling explanation is available. Men simply expect and fear that other men will be disinterested and reject them, based on what they have experienced among their peers. What truth there is in the homophobia hypothesis may lie in the perception of some men that the only man who would take a real interest in them must be sexually motivated. When Tom backs down from picking up the phone to call Dave, even if he is homophobic, he is probably less afraid that Dave will make a pass at him and more afraid that Dave won't even care that he called.

In contrast to the threat that this subculture presents to deep and lasting relationships among men, loyalty is the hallmark of true friendship. King David said, "I will have none but the most loyal as my friends" (Ps 101:6). Convenience is the great enemy of friendship. Inconvenience is seen as a bad thing in our culture. We have convenience stores, remote controls, and automatic *everything*. In the parable of the friend who knocked at midnight, Jesus points out that even if it is rather inconvenient to get up, unlock your house, and find the food required, yet because the one who knocks is a friend he will receive what he asked for. A friend is loyal at all times, not just when it's convenient, or when you happen to be having a good time together.

MAN AS PRIEST

The priest keeps things covered. No, not covered up but covered. Men find joy in covering. The consumer believes that there is satisfaction in uncovering. "Take it off." "Tell us your deepest and darkest secrets," the talk show hosts say on *Geraldo, Donahue, Oprah,* and *Sally Jessy Raphael.* More than one police show has made it on the air by sneaking a peek at the misfortunes of others. But the priest keeps things covered. He has no room for gossip, tales, and the rumors which keep *People* magazine, the talk shows, and crime shows in business. He knows the difference between discovery and exploitation.

The priest keeps things covered but not through denial. He practices intercession both before God and with those who need to learn mercy and forgiveness. The priest keeps the channels clear and the good faith between people flowing. The priest never diminishes the size of a sin, but seeks to increase the size of the repentance and mercy. By making sure that each infraction is forgiven and cleansed, the priest covers. The priest wants history to be spotless and clean so that God's decontamination will be complete. To this end, each priest adds his own style and flair. Men find covering very satisfying.

MAN AS LOVER

"Love covers a multitude of sins," Scripture tells us. Man as lover is in harmony with man as priest because both cover. In a limited sense, a lover can refer to a man's sexual passion, but the lover is much more than sexual in his love of the beloved. Perhaps because of the strength of love, it highlights each man's style more than any other role can. The greatest attribute of the lover is his fearlessness. Perfect love casts out fear, Scripture says, so the lover is more fearless than even the warrior.

The lover is known by what and who he loves. The good lover loves the giver more than the gift, God more than life, the woman more than sex, the child more than results. The lover celebrates life without fear, freely giving life and strength to others. The lover pursues, embraces, laughs, releases, and then pursues again. In all these movements, he includes the elements of his own style that will please him and his loves. The man is lover to boy and girl, grandmother and grandfather, dog and cat, and, in time, his bride and wife.

The boy cannot be a lover because he thinks too much of his

own needs, feelings, and satisfaction. Having learned that his own need and satisfaction is on the same level with that of another frees the man to be a lover by appreciating both his own feelings and those of his love.

MAN AS WARRIOR

The men's movement has brought with it the return of the warrior, this time not as a destroyer but as a defender. Their warrior is the heroic one in epic stories and poems, Gilgamesh and Hercules, not G.I. Joe and Rambo. But clever as Ulysses was with the Cyclops and as inspiring as myths can be, Gordon Dalbey probably got closer to the truth when he said that the warrior carries the sword of truth.

Ultimately the warrior knows that there are things more important than his own life, some value greater than himself. The warrior ultimately seeks a king or prophet to outlive him should his own life be lost in the struggle for what is greater than himself. The boy will always seek his own survival as the greatest good because that is the boy's task. Men must consider others as well as themselves, or they will end up fighting out of greed, revenge, or the desire to gain advantage. That is not the warrior, but an assassin at work. It is the killer boy who lives by fear, never knowing the greater power of love. Whether he is an inner city gang member, Ku Klux Klansman, or the driver who swerves into another's lane to show his anger, it is the killer boy at work.

King Saul's son Jonathan was as delightful an example of the warrior as we will ever see. He protected his friends and served his God more than family loyalty or ambition. He never fought to prove his power, yet he would take on an entire army with just his armor bearer for support when he had God to guide him.

The apostle Paul tells us that we who serve the Mighty Warrior must ourselves fight, but not against mere flesh and blood, rather against the evil of the age we live in, the dark imposter who would destroy lives and mock our King.

MAN AS KING

Every man, slave or free, poor or rich, has his area of dominion. Wisdom literature is full of instructions for kings. The prospect of a fool becoming king is too horrible to describe, according to the ancients. Much of our dominion is shared with others. The more exclusive our dominion and the higher we rise in power, the more our kingdom reflects our style, values, and investment. If earlier generations erred in asserting their dominion too rigidly, this generation has forgotten what it means to be king and see to it that justice and truth prevail in their domain.

David, who was distinctly a king said, "I will sing of your love and justice.... I will walk in my house with blameless heart.... No one who practices deceit will dwell in my house; no one who speaks falsely will stand in my presence" (Ps 101:1, 2, 7). Even if one's kingdom is no bigger than one's own home, the king rules. What I mean by that is the king insures that the values worth dying for can live in his kingdom.

This is quite different than what a boy king would seek. The boy king would want ruling to give him his own way. That is terrible and oppressive domination. Only a man is ready to be king. A man's rule seeks values greater than his own life and provision for others as well as himself. He protects and cares for the widow, orphan, and the poor.

In his own home a man may have dominion alone until he marries. After that he shares it with his wife and later his children. Sharing dominion is clearly a man-sized task. No boy could consider all the needs involved in such a position of authority. The man who has never been a boy is even more lost, for he does not even know himself.

Being king demands a certain style from the man, for to rule well is to express well the deeper values inside. The passion of a poet and the wisdom of the sage are fitting in a king and well satisfying.

MAN AS HUSBAND

While it is not recommended for all men, one manly role is that of husband. The call to be a husband is the most intense human expression of the task of being a man. If you recall, a man is to consider the needs of others as equal to his own. Nowhere is that task more passionately practiced than in marriage, where the two become one. Not only must the man consider the needs, satisfaction, and feelings of another person, but he faces a woman who is not like him in many ways and hard to figure out. On top of that, he must meet her needs as he would his own at a very intimate level and in almost every aspect of life. That is no small challenge. One shudders to think of the disaster that would follow if a boy attempted to do such a thing. Beyond that, suppose an unweaned boy who did not even understand what satisfied his needs tried to get married. *Kyrie Eleison!* Lord, have mercy!

MAN AS SERVANT

The servant is the expression of a deep and satisfying understanding of the needs of others. Like the wise virgins of the Apocalypse, servants have covered their own needs and are ready to attend to others. In Christian hierarchies, the more people you rule over, the more people you must serve. The boy cannot serve in this way for he will mistakenly conclude that serving makes him the lesser, not as important as the one being served. Whether it is P.G. Woodhouse's masterful butler Jeves or Mother Teresa of Calcutta, the distinguished servant is known by his or her understanding of the master's needs and wishes. The style of service has been perfected by long hours of practice so that the complex now appears effortless. The servant's pride is in his intimate knowledge of the master's needs ensuring that preparations have been made before the request comes.

Jesus had such style in serving that even under the duress of knowing he would be tortured to death within hours, he could say, "In my Father's house are many mansions. I go to prepare a place for you." Now that is room service with style!

PUTTING IT TOGETHER

In all these roles man is man. Each role allows a man to express another aspect of who he is and what he can be. While one man may fit one role better or feel out of place in another, all these roles, with the exception of the husband, should be explored by all men as they grow older. A man does not become a role, but the role is one dance he can learn, one tune he can sing, one job he can do, one further expression of the life within him.

It is really quite exciting when men begin to develop a repertoire of these roles for themselves. Don always dreaded visits by his in-laws. By the end of two days the house was a mess and tension reigned supreme. It soon degenerated into feigned politeness between adults, while his in-laws criticized their daughter and her children—her decisions, tastes, and vocabulary. They were quick to point out how lucky she was to have married Don. He really did not appreciate their support.

Don wanted to be a warrior and throw Dad and Mom out of the house, but that did not seem right with the family. So he turned into a servant instead. He waited on his wife and her parents to try and make them more comfortable and agreeable. However, they used this opportunity to reinforce to their daughter how *extraordinarily* lucky she was to have found such a husband. In return for his service, his wife served him up a stare that would freeze a dinosaur.

Don then turned to the role of a priest. He wanted to cover his wife by helping her deal with the problems that came to the surface whenever her parents visited. Yet she was not very open to this approach when her parents came to visit; although several problems were covered, overall, she felt that he was siding with her parents against her.

It was only after talking with a friend that Don began to realize that he was king in his home. The rules in his kingdom were for him and his queen to set, including how visitors were to treat the queen. "Your parents may be visiting royalty," he told his wife, "but we are the responsible rulers here. Whatever happens in our house we have to answer for and not your parents."

The very next visit the situation changed. There were no confrontations, no laying down the law, just simple statements like, "That is not how we handle criticism here. We encourage the person to do better." The very fact that the king and queen knew that it was their home and their hospitality changed patterns profoundly. The values worth dying for began to live in their kingdom.

The different roles a man uses to give life can blend together at times. They harmonize well with the roles for women and children. Picking the right one for the occasion really satisfies a man and gives him a sense of style. By now we know how important that satisfaction is to a man and how life-giving his repertoire of roles can be to others.

But how does a man go about becoming a father? Is it simply a matter of biology?

NINE

Becoming a Father

"YES," HE SAID, PEERING INTO MY MOUTH, "if all is going well, I'm becoming a father right now." Somehow he didn't seem as excited as he should be.

"Open wide," he said, and I did. Phil had always been a strange dentist, but this definitely topped it. When I came in, he would hand me a teddy bear, stuff suction tubes in my mouth, and then talk non-stop.

"Yeah, my wife is in England getting pregnant right now. We tried for years and finally had to go the in-vitro way. It turns out," he said, looking for something behind my molar, "that it is cheaper to fly to London and get it done there than to pay the doctors here. I would have gone along, but someone had to pay for the trip." With that he took out his handy-dandy air-and-water sprayer and aimed it at my face, instead of inside my mouth. I ended up with water all over my face.

"Oh! Did I miss again? I must be out of practice!"

"Hhaaurr eeyyuuu wwea quii aaaa!" I answered as his little suction tube grabbed ahold of my tongue. (Translated that means, "Sure you are! Quit that!") I'd never been with a man when he was becoming a father before!

Phil was clearly pleased. "You know, if you were burned up in a plane crash, I wouldn't need X-rays to identify these teeth," he said. Then he drifted back to his main theme and filled in some details. "She just stays in a hotel room until they have succeeded. She should be back in a couple of weeks. Who knows, maybe I'm a dad right now!"

"Chhoongaauuaaheunn!" I told him, and meant every bit of it. (Translated that means, "Congratulations.")

The average man comes to the moment of becoming a father a bit differently than Phil did. There is a mystical passage for a man the moment he discovers he is now the source of new life. Not every man will recognize and seize the moment, but for those who do the universe momentarily disappears and then returns with a penetrating brilliance. History is inexorably changed for him and the whole world, for who knows what this new life will bring? This sounds the starting gun beginning the great race for which he has trained all his life.

As a boy he learned to express his feelings and meet his own needs. In time his father introduced him to the wide world of satisfaction and exertion. In twelve short years, he became a master at knowing himself and faced the challenge of leaving behind the identity he had just mastered for a new one. While keeping all that before him, he had learned as a young man from the community of men about his history and how he was to be a part of the future. Now he was a man. Shakily at first, but with rising strength, this man had learned to meet others' needs along with his own. Fairness and hard bargains became the rule. He now knew how to protect and serve. Once again, no sooner had he mastered this identity when something deep, unfulfilled, frightening, and yet good began to tear apart the man he knew himself to be. The desire to give life began to challenge him to be more then he had ever known. He wished to become a father.

All his life the mystery of the father had pulled at him calling for something beyond bargaining and fairness, something that gave without being repaid. This was a strange path. It led towards paying another's bills, even suffering for things one didn't do and for things one didn't deserve. To do all this with satisfaction is the secret joy of being a father. This he now wanted for himself. Does it sound familiar to you?

Becoming a father has become less about children and more

about marriage or the lack of it as unwed parents and divorces have proliferated. Furthermore, childbirth increasingly ties fathers to Lamaze classes and the community of women, with fewer ties to the fellowship of men. Yet becoming a father is a male event, participated in only by men, never in the absence of women, of course. From sheer folly and ignorance becoming a dad is often viewed as what ties a man and woman together, rather than what ties a father and child together. (I make the point only in contrast to the prevalent view, because having a baby is the highest expression of the life-giving properties in both men and women.)

There is a general undercurrent of belief in society that men are not drawn to fatherhood as strongly as women feel the call to motherhood. Some people feel that women want to get married and have children, but men like to roam and have sex. Yet it is my contention that any man who does not become a father in some meaningful way is doomed to a life of unfulfilled misery. He becomes an airplane that never flew, a ship that never sailed, a racehorse that stayed in the stable, an aborted birth. Imagine building a house for twenty years and then not moving into it, preparing twenty-five years for the Olympics and then not competing in your event. Such a tragedy would probably warrant its own made-for-TV movie. Such is the fate of the man who fails to become a father.

To be a father is to give without receiving in return. All men are destined to be fathers and will remain frustrated, unhappy, and unfulfilled if they do not reach this calling. Unlike the gangster mentality, I do not mean a man must get a woman pregnant; that never yet made a man a father. All men have within them the need to be the source of life to others and to give without seeking to receive—this is what it really means to be a father. It is the giving of life which every man must experience. Otherwise, he condemns himself to a miserable, unfulfilled existence. It is not enough to give life randomly, like some tomcat pursuing a queen in heat and then disappearing when his job is done. One needs to do so with personal commitment and expense over enough time to see new life grow—the preferred minimum length of time being just a lifetime. Anything less and a man feels diminished.

Without something to give, a father becomes a eunuch on a honeymoon. It is in the strain and effort, and even the failures in fathering, that the really best parts of a man are revealed, tested, and strengthened. For this reason, the father welcomes the suffering and cost to himself.

Why does the athlete compete? Why does the actor anxiously wait for the curtain to go up? Why is the Indy 500 driver eager for the green flag? Why does the salesman gear up for a big presentation? Why does the mountain climber seek Everest? The answer to all these challenges is the same—because it will bring out the best in him. Yes, deep within each person is the burning desire to see what is best in him or her on display—tested, tried, demonstrated, and tangible. It is the desire to be known mixed with the call of glory. Only being a father can bring out what is the very best in a man.

And what torments these contestants endure to demonstrate the best they have. Race drivers crash, burn, break bones, and come back from the hospital to drive again. Football players take to the field with broken bones. Mountain climbers lose their fingers and toes to frostbite. Gymnasts and skaters give up their entire social lives for years of grueling practice on the mat or the ice. Actors live in their vans and borrow money until their friends and relatives can hardly stand to see their tired faces, yet they persevere. All these contestants in the game of life endure hardship for the chance to discover and display what is best about themselves.

Suppose a great Russian weight lifter stood backstage after a lifetime of training, sniffed the acrid jolting shot of ammonia, and walked out to the weight room confident that he could set a new world's record. As he stood before the judges and audience, the judges told him, "Weight lifting is no longer of any value and will not be allowed. You are a Russian. Dance like Nureyev." If compelled to dance, he would be humiliated and laughed to scorn, for dancing will not display what is best in him. Yet Nureyev would have felt, in an instant, that dancing would bring out his best while lifting weights would not.

Find a man who has no opportunity to express what is best about him and you will find a despondent, irritable, restless, unfulfilled, and miserable man. It is worth noting that this desire is not about competition. What really satisfies is the chance to show what is best about us in a way that can be seen. When it is eclipsed by another who is greater than ourselves, we become invisible and unhappy. When our skill is far better than the competition but we do not achieve our best, we find no joy. Take the man who plays tennis against a far inferior player and wins with no effort; he will have less satisfaction in winning than he would in losing by a narrow margin to anyone seeded at Wimbledon. Satisfaction comes from expressing what is best in us.

The boy trains to meet his needs, the man trains to meet his needs and those of others. This prepares him to have a self—a big strong self. He is a person in history, full of life. He is now ready to run the good race, fight the good fight, dance the great dance, he is ready to give life. Only in giving life will he find the deepest, most satisfying expression of what is best about himself. This is the main event. This is the real man at his best. To do so earns him the title of *Father,* a title that would mean nothing if it did not express the very best of him.

Life is a mystery. What makes one frog alive and another dead? What makes a tree alive and a board not? What makes a flower burst out of a seed? We do not know; it is a mystery. To think that life might spring up where there was none before compels us to look at spring leaves or follow Jesus to Lazarus' tomb. And when a man has found that he can bring life into being, it is the most godlike feeling that he can experience without sinning. It is the very best part of him.

STORIES OF FATHERS

My friend Rick helped me see how this worked. He had a twelve-year-old daughter when he and his wife conceived again. Together we all shared the excitement for about three months.

Then the baby died. Rick's wife miscarried as far as the doctors were concerned, but to Rick, his baby died. He mourned for over a year. To this day he gets tears in his eyes when I ask him about it. One morning over breakfast he said to me, "You know, my feelings about my baby are a little bit selfish. Part of what hurt so much is that being a father brings out the best in me. These are the deepest, strongest feelings I know. And then, to have it all torn away...."

Rick's father had not known the deep satisfaction and joy Rick knew. As he grew up, Rick's dad had told him, "Don't be like me." In fact, he seemed to think that the best thing he could do for Rick was to leave his son alone and let as little as possible of himself rub off on the boy. To this man being a father only showed up the worst things about himself.

Travis, my cousin, was looking for a safe and normal life when he had an experience similar to Rick's. One terrible morning he and his wife woke up to find their only child had died of crib death. As we sat by the window looking out at the San Gabriel Mountains, he told me, "When that happened it changed my life forever." Travis changed careers, lifestyle, and even who he was. Later, as I watched him hug a young bereaved mother, I could see the best in him still looking for a way to be expressed.

Mark has a similar story. His son Jonathan had Down's Syndrome and after a short life died from medical complications. Mark was inconsolable with pain. Some of the best of him was cut down in its prime. Mark was a teacher. He knew that Jonathan would need the best of his teaching abilities to make it in the world. What Mark knew best was how to fit into a world that thought he was different and would never fully accept him no matter what he did. This quality marked the very best part of Mark. He took all that he treasured and poured it into his son and the plans he had for his son. When Jonathan died some of the deepest and best parts of Mark died too.

Mark found the best part of himself as a father, Travis found his deepest understanding, and Rick felt his potential to love. The tragic contrast between Rick and his father points out the difference between men who have learned that they have something to give and those who haven't. Rick had something to give and knew that fatherhood would bring it into full view. He was ready to run the race he had trained for his whole life. Even those bleak days with his own father had helped him see the importance of what a father needed to give.

The truth of the matter goes beyond one lifetime, however, because fatherhood is an eternal business, at least for the righteous. Unlike the marriage bond, which is temporal and endures on a good run until "death do us part," paternity is an eternal arrangement. The parent-and-child relationship is still valid in heaven; otherwise, the promise to Abraham that he will be the father of many nations is a meaningless gesture. In fact we see that it is true when Jesus tells us that after Lazarus died, he was comforted by Father Abraham. What endures eternally is the life-giving family line, not the biological family. Entrance into eternal life is predicated on receiving and giving life.

THE COST OF FATHERHOOD

These eternal bonds between father and child are neither easy nor cheap. For just those reasons they are all the more meaningful to the man who possesses them with understanding. In some ways, they cost the father his very life, whether you measure that in time, energy, or resources. The cost of giving without receiving in return is a kind of dying. With each sacrifice, the father must die a bit and rejoice that he was worthy of glory.

Becoming a father is paradoxically a dying process, as are all passages. The new father must leave behind his old understanding of who he is if he is to participate in something new. Most dads do this joyfully, but with a bit of apprehension and fear thrown in. This is the first passage for which the man must pay the cost himself.

The first cost of fatherhood is the man's possessive enjoyment of his wife. If he has been blessed, his wife has been his garden of delights and he, her lover—the object of her devoted love. Yet, when she becomes pregnant, her body, mind, and feelings turn to another, a beloved stranger. This stranger can keep her awake nights when such attempts by her husband would meet with an angry rebuke. He becomes an escort and support, almost an understudy in his wife's heart. There is little that is his alone anymore. He must begin to learn again that intimacy is for a time and place and not diminished by being shared.

The newborn emerges from the very privacy which once the father called his exclusive domain and he would likely kill anyone else who dared enter there. The child once emerged lays claim to his wife's breasts, once his alone, and takes over without a care in the world about the father's feelings. For the father who was first a boy and then a man, even this disregard will bring joy, for he knows how much better it is to give than to receive.

It is the cost that lets us know that someone loves us. When someone has a good time for us, it doesn't count for much. If someone is willing to suffer for us, then we pay attention. The gift of being a father is to give without return, to suffer what you would not have had to suffer on behalf of someone else. In doing so, the father makes an example of God the Father's love which is understandable to his own children. It is not in contrast to the mother that he does so, but in concert with her.

While being a father is a man's greatest expression of himself, he is still pushed beyond his limits. When men are stretched to new lengths, they also need encouragement. There was a time when all a man needed to say was, "We are expecting a child," and friends and colleagues would pump his hand and fill his ears with congratulations. That isn't the reaction anymore. Passing out cigars to your cheering friends is becoming rare. When a man announces that his wife is pregnant, people say, "Did you want it?" or, "Can you afford it?" or, "Are you going to keep it?" Is this good news or not? The politically correct response is to ask if the child is wanted before congratulating. From there the discussion usually turns to the enormous cost. Having babies costs a lot. Raising children is expensive. Dad is supposed to pay the bill, although that is less and less the case. Mom shares the load too. What is lacking in this discussion is the encouragement and joy needed to help a man be all that he can be.

The father longs for the opportunity to demonstrate his love. He is eager to fight the good fight because it shows the best of who he is. As his child grows, the opportunities increase. As his child grows older, he has something more to provide. Each level of his child's development brings out more of the best of him. The opportunities afforded the father's heart by his children let him become more than he ever thought he could become. His children will find in him more than he ever knew he contained. Sons and daughters will each bring out different aspects of the best of him, as will their differing personalities.

Yet realistically, not everything that comes out of fathers under the strain of growing is wonderful and life-giving. Growing and stretching also means exposing hidden inadequacies. When a man comes to the time when he is called on to produce the best part of himself and then finds it to be crippled or disfigured, the usual response is one of rage, shame, and distance either through withdrawal or intimidation. The rage of feeling disqualified for the race he trained for all his life can make a man into truly bad company. Equally devastating is the fear of being disqualified which keeps men, like Rick's dad, from even entering the race to begin with. Yet if there is a dark side to the father who stumbles across his crippling rage, he can find healing for the wounded boy inside himself if he will persevere and face the pain.

Building on previous chapters, let's now explore the relationship between a father and his children.

TEN

Fathers and Their Children

... The essential attribute of the macho—power—almost always reveals itself as a capacity for wounding, humiliating, annihilating. Nothing is more natural, therefore, than [the man's] indifference toward the offspring he engenders. He is not the founder of a people; he is not a patriarch who exercises patria potestas; *he is not a king or a judge or a chieftain of a clan. He is power isolated in its own potency, without relationship or compromise with the outside world. He is pure incommunication, a solitude that devours itself and everything it touches. He does not pertain to our world; he is not from our city; he does not live in our neighborhood. He comes from far away: he is always far away. He is the Stranger.[1]*

Octavio Paz
The Labyrinth of Solitude

I N HIS CLASSICAL STATEMENT of the male worldview, Octavio Paz has provided a definition of masculinity in his Latin culture. Men exist in a labyrinth of solitude. "We are alone," he says, "solitude, the source of anxiety, begins on the day we are deprived of maternal protection and fall into a strange and hostile world."[2] So men resort instead to "the pistol, a phallic symbol that discharges death rather than life..."[3]

Man is seen as death-giving, father is death-giving, even humor is death-giving, bringing unexpected annihilation, dust, and nothingness. Power is measured by the ability to destroy and consume. Little wonder that the child deprived of maternal protection is plunged into anxiety, if this is the nature of the father. Millions of people hold this view of fathers or variations on it.

Contrasting with this view of the father as indifferent or even hostile to his children is the image of the father described by the Old Testament prophet Zephaniah (see Zeph 3:17). He is a father who is among his children, like a warrior keeping them safe, singing songs over them, quieting each one with his love, and exulting over them with shouts of joy. This father is no stranger. Instead, he is pure communication. He gives life, not death.

EXPLORING THE FATHER BOND

But which of these views is the truth about fathers? Which is more realistic? Which behavior can we expect from a father? It is not unusual for psychologists and therapists to argue against the view that fathers are by nature deeply bonded to their children. Therapists might not go as far as Paz with his definition of the masculine soul, but they often seem to believe that men have to "get in touch with their feminine side" in order to bond with their children and develop a nurturing role. There is a widespread view that men who do not embrace their feminine side and, in addition, reject masculine proclivities should never be allowed around children. In this view, held unconsciously by many professionals, men are pure isolation, with a sex and power drive thrown in. Being exposed to this sort of "masculine" influence is precisely the fear that torments the children "deprived of maternal protection" in the isolated world Paz describes.

Yet, if this destructive nature is not authentic masculinity in action but the rage of men with broken bonds, then men who do bond well in the masculine way will resemble Zephaniah's description of a father's love. What I mean is this: if you stick your finger in a man's eye, he will usually get mad. If you hit a man in the most private part of his body, you can expect him to get very unpleasant, even violent, when he is in a position to retaliate. The fact is, if you cause a man pain for a long time, especially where it hurts the most, he may become very hostile towards everyone. Thus, a man separated from his deepest source of satisfaction, meaning, and love may become destructive to himself and others in his life. If this is true then deeply bonded men should be less hostile, destructive, and angry.

I see one example of this kind of father bond each Tuesday morning at six when Wayne shows up at a prayer breakfast with his adoptive daughter Melissa. (It used to be a men's prayer breakfast; now it is a prayer breakfast.) Melissa is only two and Wayne is too old to really care about his next birthday party. Wayne is a farmer's son from Iowa, fixes his own cars, and teaches math. He is not a man known for being deeply in touch with his feelings, and Melissa is not biologically related to him, this side of Noah, that is.

At the breakfast Melissa crawls up on Daddy's lap, putting her arms around his neck, and curls up for ten to fifty minutes. Occasionally, she will poke or swat Dean, who usually sits next to Wayne and who asks her dumb questions, or she will fuss about her orange juice. Wayne takes Melissa to parent-and-child play times at Cal State University, where he is usually the only father present. Wayne is a pacifist, hardly ever loses his temper, and opposes the death penalty. He is a little unusual, yet most of us know someone like Wayne. Is he an aberration?

Rick is home with Ryan. Like Wayne he takes to fathering like a duck to water. When he drops Ryan off at the play area in the fitness center, Ryan often clings to him for a while. This behavior mystifies the women that run the center. Why would this little boy cling to his father? Rick says that it was worth having his business go bad to have this time with his son. No one has ever seen him be violent or abusive.

Bob, whose father is also his grandfather, came home to find his wife in bed with her boss. He did not try to kill the other man. Bob is not affluent and his health is not great, but his loyalty to his children makes it hard for him to leave the situation without finding a way to care for them.

In a similar but even sadder situation, Dr. Sam slept for months on the couch after his wife threw him out of the bedroom to make room for her boyfriends. Dr. Sam was raised in orphanages and foster homes and found it almost impossible to think of leaving his own children no matter what his wife did. Sam had his doctorate in psychology, but that did little to help. After all, the last half century of psychology has done little more for the father than what Paz described. Sam eventually found a safe home for himself and his children. He continues to be a quiet, even-tempered man.

If it were only an academic issue, it would not matter what a father's bond is towards his children. But it is my contention that this bond is the main event for all males. Without it men are doomed to unhappiness. At the risk of being run out of town as a heretic, I might even say that fatherhood and motherhood are more the point of our life than religion. God did not tell the pair in the garden to meditate on his words, sing worshipfully, or play the harp, but rather to multiply and fill the earth: dad-and-mom stuff.

This father bond looks different at each age of the child and is different with each child. Father bonds are somewhat different with sons and daughters, or first and last children, but they are more alike than they are different. It may even be that men bond more readily than women, although that view will probably surprise most readers. In fact, that opinion will be vigorously contested by many who will quote experiences with men like Paz described.

Perhaps the existence of so many men in the macho category suggests that they are more prone to bonding than they appear to be. If so much effort must be exerted to prevent bonding, and if men insulate themselves from pain so strongly, it suggests to me that men are hiding a point of great vulnerability and pain. Only someone with a tendency to bond would have to work so hard to prevent it.

In any conflict the combatants seek to cover up their areas of vulnerability. If men are most vulnerable in the area of their bonds, and primarily their bonds to their children, then men who wish to avoid the kind of pain that Bob and Dr. Sam experienced must find ways to stay disconnected from their children. To do that they must clutter up or even destroy the bonding surface so nothing will stick.

Incidentally, the sexual and marital bond is also very important to men and can also be a source of great pain when broken or damaged. To avoid hurts in this area, the same strategies can be employed to clutter up or destroy the bonding surface. It appears that both Dr. Sam's and Bob's wives were busy preventing any bonding sexually with their husbands. They did this, as many men do, by copulating indiscriminately. There is nothing like lots of matings to prevent bonding.

A parent, in this case a dad, will likely stay bonded with his children up until the age when they are recapitulating the highest level of his own growth. So, let us say that Dad got through the first two, three, or four of Erikson's crises as a boy and then got stuck. Dad will still bond but in an impaired way. He will enjoy closeness with his child until the youngster begins to navigate the same problem that obstructed the father's growth. In a very real sense, a dad must review and even pass through all the developmental stages with each of his children in order to maintain the bond. Once the child reaches the stage of the father's defeat, Dad must confront the crisis again, but now successfully, in order to keep the bond with the child intact and healthy. If he turns away, Dad is faced with the choice of letting his pain cause him to withdraw from the child and break the bond, or else he will cripple the child to insure that he and child do not go farther in their growth. It is the strength of this parental bond that has caused many fathers to go through the pain of recovery. Often, this bond with their children is the only bond strong enough to keep these wounded fathers from running away.

Take, for instance, Joe. He was the perfect father until Joey was old enough to sleep in his own bed. Joe played and laughed, while Joey played with his bottle, learned to crawl, stood on his own, and learned to walk and talk. Joe was patient and enjoyed helping his son, even when Joey couldn't succeed. When Joey was scared at nights and wanted comfort, Joe got him out of his crib and brought him to bed. But one day Joey turned three. By that time he slept in his own bed and wandered in to his parents' room whenever he felt the need at night. Joe found himself telling Joey sharply that now that he was three he needed to stay in his own bed all night. He would have added, "and don't cry," but he didn't believe that boys should not cry so he stopped before he said it.

The first bad night that brought Joey wandering into his parents' bedroom after that brought surprising anger and frustration out of Joe. His wife said, "What's gotten into you? You never used to be so harsh. Now you scared him." Joe was surprised at himself, but he said, "He has to learn to stay in his own bed."

A bit of history would reveal that Joe's father had become sick at the same time that Joe's younger brother was born, just after Joe himself turned three. What had been a pleasant childhood became rather unforgiving, as irritable parents tried to cope with tough times. In order to continue being the kind of father he was meant to be, Joe had to heal and correct his own distortions about being three. Without his son's tears, Joe would have run from his pain and played "hardball" with his son. Joe decided instead to face the truth about his parent's limitations and his own pain. Then he was able to discover, along with Joey, what a three-year-old boy really wants and needs in the middle of the night.

This sort of father is best described as an overcomer. He is motivated by love for his children to face the pain of his own developmental deficiencies and stay bonded to them as they continue to grow.

Much more common is the man who will not bond because he fears the pain. We have already talked about pain in the chapter about myths and men. For fathers, the beliefs about men and pain begin to take their toll as they are forced to decide whether life is about avoiding pain or facing it with whatever determination they have. The man who fails to see the value of pain can best avoid it by keeping his bonding surfaces cluttered with what I call junk bonds. He can love his car, his sports on TV, his fishing or golf, his booze, his work, his religion, or his neighbor's wife. But he neglects his own wife and children, as well as other significant relationships.

Men who believe that they are not the bonding type will not even try to be close to their wife or children. These are the men who Paz so aptly describes. Their lives are cluttered with junk bonds. Perhaps the best known of these bonds are those to gangs, organized crime, military and para-military groups, hate organizations, travel, and even law enforcement. Musicians have no shortage of music about the non-bonding man who thinks of no one but himself. He is often viewed as a type of man rather than the aberration he truly is.

Doug loved motorcycles and dirt bikes. He had loved the power and control and thrill ever since he was twelve years old. Doug's dad was a self-made millionaire and their relationship was distant. When Doug's son was born and took all his wife's attention away from him, Doug went back to dirt bikes and demanding more sex from his wife when he was home. He did everything he could to keep from bonding with his son and feeling the pain of how distant his relationship had been and still was with his own father. He even hung pictures of dirt bikes in the bedroom where most fathers might put pictures of their sons. He was keeping his bonding surface covered with junk.

Conversely, men who believe that they must become feminized in order to bond with their children will be greatly frustrated in their attempts to be more like a woman. Women compound this problem by supporting the idea that a good father should bond with a child in exactly the same way as a mother does, and so provide a "back up" for Mom when she is too tired, overwhelmed, or busy. Further, when neither of the parents has seen a functional father in action, anyone's guesses go about what a father should be like.

Yet, the road to fatherhood is not found through well meaning advice but through seeking satisfaction. For fathers, satisfaction is found by bringing out the best in themselves and giving without receiving in return, in addition to the many other things that satisfy boys and men. This search allows input from the man himself, his wife, children, friends, relatives, and even his children's friends.

Men who believe that bonding should be painless will seek to change and control everyone they bond with to insure that they do not experience pain, anxiety, or loss in their relationships. These bonds can be strong, but they are based on fear and serve to insure that the child never outgrows the parent emotionally. Perhaps this is the most common sort of father. He bonds sufficiently to maintain control but avoids the painful parts of his life where change is needed, unless his wife leaves him or his children provoke him to it. Mostly, he tries to keep everyone in order without ever asking himself if keeping it that way satisfies him or anyone.

Glen was this way. He was always careful to be right, disciplined his children, told them what they should do without really asking for their input, and pointed out all their mistakes. His children loved him, feared him, were loyal to him, and kept him at a respectful distance all their lives.

As the father's own development will affect his fathering differently at each stage of the child's growth, we should take time to examine what it is like to be a father as one's children grow up.

THE HEALTHY FATHER AND
THE UNWEANED CHILD

New fathers enter what Ken Canfield of the National Center for Fathering calls the age of idealism when their children are first born. Due in part to widespread success in achieving the first stage of development, most parents are able to freely join in with their children at this point. Such a bond produces joy and delight between the father and child. Naturally, the father who did not bond with his parents even at this point in his own development will be very poor at parenting himself. He will lack an internal understanding of how things work at this stage and suffer severe levels of emotional pain.

During the first four years of a child's life, the growth and rate of change is enormous. The good dad delights in this growth by observing it carefully and encouraging each new step. This is the kind of attention described by John Fischer in his song, "Christopher's Toes."

> Christopher knows Christopher's toes
> He just found them today
> Stuck in the air at the end of his chair
> Ten little toes just waitin' to play.[4]

Not only do children discover their toes but their tongues and voices, and inevitably they discover Dad's nostrils are just the right size for little fingers with fingernails that should have been trimmed. It is a time when little ones discover their senses and muscles. For the father this is also a time of getting to know his child. It is a time for play and mutual discovery. Dad wants to know what his baby can do. Being together is the key to success. The more time spent together the greater the discoveries. Since this stage of life is usually exhausting for the mother with late night feedings, time spent with Dad is a welcome respite for her. It also allows both parents to revel in the life they are building together. This is a new form of intimacy for parents who are not used to being that close when a third person is involved. Mom, Dad, and baby are learning what it means to be a family.

Knowing his child becomes a form of rediscovering the world and himself for the father. It is a chance to enrich his sense of the world which may have languished since his own childhood. In revisiting a child's world, the father will experience a feeling much like falling in love with his son or daughter. This rush of experience and feeling occurs as everything becomes new and alive again and is tempered by the exhaustion that most parents experience in the early years of childrearing in a culture that tends to isolate parents from other support.

The father who was raised in relative isolation and never participated in raising children must overcome his early years spent alone and his limited sense of self. Repulsion with diapers, fear of holding babies, and reluctance to coo and snuggle must be overcome to form a close relationship with his newborn. This is all part of the discovery of himself and the world that the first-time father experiences. With each new baby, the father is able to focus more acutely on the uniqueness of that child. In its own way this provides a needed balance, for the father learns more with his first child about being a dad. This unique bond requires more time to produce. What the father learns with his first child prepares him to appreciate his later children more precisely for who each of them is, so he can meet their needs more accurately even with less time available per child.

THE WOUNDED FATHER AND
THE UNWEANED CHILD

The father whose own development crashed at the unweaned stage is faced with a monumental task in raising children. He will either prove to be neglectful and distant or overprotective in a controlling way when relating with his children. This overprotectiveness is many times the source of or results in emotional and physical abuse directed toward controlling the child. A father who was sexually abused at this stage will typically experience his desire to bond with his child, whether male or female, as a sexual impulse. Closeness of any kind for him must involve sexual activity and may result in repeating the abuse or rigidly removing himself from his children in angry isolation.

While it is unlikely that any severe abuse at this age will be corrected without a great amount of pain and healing, most fathers discover only mild deficits that require them to overcome their discomfort, anxiety, and embarrassment at entering the baby's world. The father who knows what satisfies him will excitedly plunge through this barrier and may soon be changing diapers, giving baths, and taking baby on walks—all with a "daddy" feel to it. In addition, he will rediscover the world with his child, feeling the joy of encountering a whole new world once again.

Wilbur was one father who did not make it through his own unweaned years intact. In fact, while his parents neither abused or neglected him in any criminal way, they treated him in the same way one might treat a prize-winning cow. He received his food regularly, his stall was clean, his pasture fenced, and he got his shots on time. The only cloud in the sky seemed so natural that he never saw it. His father and mother worked hard but never stopped to find him interesting. As a result, it never occurred to him that he or, later, his six children were the least bit interesting. This might seem odd in a man with a doctorate in counseling, but these things happen.

Each child received his or her food regularly, each was always squeaky clean, and each one got his or her shots on time. He never thought to notice the gifts his children brought him or to compliment them on what they made in school. He didn't think to play with their toes or fingers, or blow on their tummies. When they grew up and got married, he never thought to ask their boyfriends or girlfriends what they liked, believed, or even where they wanted to live.

At his retirement party, many students from his school claimed he had been a guiding influence on them—after all it was his job and he worked hard—but his own children did not all attend. Some even declared they had no tribute to give. Wilbur didn't seem to notice. He didn't see why his children should be interested in him, anyway. He expressed no need or feeling and sought no satisfaction from his children. He simply cared for them with the dispassionate interest that seemed right because that's how he had been raised.

Due to the interest shown by some family friends, some of Wilbur's children began to express their needs and feelings. Soon the family began to disintegrate, although Wilbur never thought to look at himself to see if he were part of the problem because he found himself totally uninteresting. The real problem was that Wilbur got lost even before he was weaned. He had no sense of being loved for who he was, no sense of being someone special.

THE HEALTHY FATHER AND THE WEANED CHILD

As weaning approaches, whether the child is still being nursed or not, the father begins to find himself increasingly teaching the child. It is the time to answer incessant "why" questions and explain everything about the world. The father who has explored the world with his child for the last several years will find these questions excite his own curiosity and add zest to life. Teaching and learning go together.

It is a time of imagination as much as a time for facts, because the child finds it easier to imagine the impossible than to understand the actual. Fantasies of being big and living in Daddy's world have special meaning. Little boys want to be like Dad and marry Mom, while little girls want to marry Dad and take better care of him than Mommy does.

This is also a time for fears to grow. As weaning approaches, the child discovers that others—usually siblings—increasingly compete for his or her coveted spot. Jealous rage, possessiveness, and a desire for exclusive relationships with one's parents characterize this age.

The healthy father takes time to teach his children about inclusive love that does not fear the other by teaching his children how to take care of themselves, pets, toys, and younger children. This is at the level of caring play and not adult responsibilities. It is sharing toys and Daddy's knee and helping little sister or brother stay on Daddy's back for a ride.

The healthy father approaches weaning his child with anticipation. Once weaned, children are able to explore the world with Dad much more freely. After the initial apprehension subsides, the child is free to pass from imagination to learning. Very soon school will begin and with it the need to understand the outside world of strangers. School is like a giant bicycle for the child to ride and master. Parents prepare each child to master these demands even when the start isn't smooth.

Fathers of weaned children help their children learn to use comparisons, rules, and competition to measure their own growth, not their own value. Expressing and demonstrating what the child has learned is subject to constant comparison; otherwise, the results are meaningless.

One key area of learning at this age involves the conscience of each child. Within a warm and strong relationship with parents, rules and examples are carefully matched to see if the rule maker follows the rule. Children discover that rules give them enormous power over adults who are stuck at this stage themselves. Without judging by satisfaction, however, rules become a method of moral control over others, rather than a way to bring out the best in us. For instance, instead of making everyone line up by height and serving in that order like they taught in school, sometimes it is more satisfying to bring Grandma her food first, so she can sit down and rest while others are being served.

Dad is the one who keeps the secret knowledge of the good things inside each of his children. With patience born of faith, he searches diligently until the good part of his child is discovered, or a lesson is learned. At these times the child learns to be more than he or she was before because not everything we discover is there before we begin the search.

It is soon apparent that Dad and Mom are not the only teachers that their child will need, but they are the main solution to the child's need to know the meaning of what they learn, particularly through comparisons. It is easy for people to see what they are not, until too much attention to the fact causes them to develop defenses that blind them. Becoming what one has not yet become is much harder to believe and hope for, especially when the new thing is too different to even understand.

Jimmy always answered questions more slowly than his class-mates. Some of them suggested that Jimmy wasn't all that smart. In fact, Jimmy was unusually bright and reflective and pondered questions before answering. His answers were often unusual as a result. When the teacher asked "If Tommy has ten apples and he takes seven from Billy and gives three to George, how many apples does he have?" Jimmy thought about why Tommy would take Billy's apples when he could have given three to George and still had seven, which is more than he could eat anyway. Unfortunately, the other kids laughed at his pauses and unusual observations. He needed his parents' help to know he was not stupid and to understand why he was dif-ferent from the other children. He needed to know it wasn't bad simply because he was slower and more thoughtful.

My older son Jamie told me once that he didn't think he could ever be the kind of father that I am, adding that he hoped that didn't go to my head. Well, it is impossible for a teenager to imagine himself raising children as well as years of diligent effort have taught me to do. What I know that he doesn't is the difference between what he knows at seventeen and what I knew when I was his age. That gives me hope that my son will one day far surpass me.

During that conversation with Jamie, he pointed out how he had not become a part of the community of men until he was well into high school. I had to admit that I had not introduced him to the community at weaning as I should and that his rite of passage into manhood had also lacked significant communal elements. These things also made him feel unprepared. When I recounted this conversation to Gordon Dalbey one evening, Gordon remarked on the advantage Jamie had in even being able to know at age seventeen that he had a deficit in his introduction to the community of men. With all this in mind, it is easy for me to tell Jamie that I have every hope and expectation that he will surpass me as a father in twenty-four years. I have the privilege of helping Jamie know what his comparisons mean.

THE WOUNDED FATHER OF THE WEANED CHILD

The father who has not navigated this time in his own childhood without mishap will not know how to guide his children through their sense of jealousy and fear. He will already have struggled with jealousy over his wife and child's bond, which may lead to weaning the child too early as well as to increased fear and jealousy by the child. Often such a father has isolated his wife from her friends, so she is more vulnerable to exhaustion and discouragement and more dependent on him. Yet he is unable to support her without anger.

In response to this crisis, the wounded father will often angrily or coldly reject his sons and foster his daughter's immature, jealous attachment to himself. In so doing he seeks to keep what his children can give for himself alone, rather than teaching them what they have to offer others. For his daughter this often means she must stay Daddy's girlfriend forever. For his son it means performing and bringing glory to his father. The son becomes a slave who cannot compete for Mother's attention with his father, except when Dad is away. This may prove a training ground for mistresses the son will have later on.

Tom was a father whose life had fallen apart during his post-weaning years. His parents took to fighting and his dad left. As time went on, he began to call his dad by his first name and treat him just like his stepdad. In reality Tom had no dad. Since, like all children at this age, you are what you learn, he learned to be his own dad. He went on to one school after another, he got degrees in religion, business, and education.

Tom married young and had three children who did well until they reached school age. From there on Tom's anger grew, he angrily compared his children with each other, he compared them with others outside the family, he compared them with the rules he had set and found them all wanting. Tom compared his wife with other women who were smarter, thinner, more pleasing, less passive, better dressed, had bigger thises and smaller thats, and were better with money. His family began to like it when he was away on business because they were tired of being yelled at and feeling angry or afraid.

Tom could not see why they simply didn't learn to be what he told them to be, what the Bible told them to be, what good psychological theory told them to be, what any intelligent person could see they should be. Had Tom ever stopped to ask he might have noticed that he was not satisfied with life, but rather than seek satisfaction he made rules and berated his family. They, in turn, learned to feel bad, sneak around his rules, counter with rules of their own, and likewise be dissatisfied. If it wouldn't make them feel so bad, they might have even wished him dead.

Meanwhile, Tom regularly became dissatisfied with his church, his friends, his job, his house, and the part of the country he lived in. He decided that he would move to a new location, dragging his unhappy family along with him. In this, he had at least improved on his own father, for he did take his children out to see the world without abandoning them. He only made them wish at times that he would.

Tom simply could not see why his family did not learn to become the people he wanted them to be. He didn't know that while it is important to produce products for your efforts, that principle works for things but not for people. In a perverse twist on a father's hope, Tom became a source of despair, seeing in his family only what they were not.

THE HEALTHY FATHER TO YOUNG MEN AND WOMEN

Contrary to popular belief, I do not believe that there is much difference between a father's relationship to his daughters and sons. The primary difference involves the way in which a father affirms his children's sexual identity. For the son the message is, "Your sexuality is like mine and that is very fine." For the daughter the message is, "Your sexuality is the opposite of mine and that is very fine." For both sexes of children, the major factor is the father's respect for his own sexuality and lack of fear of theirs.

The father of young men and women enjoys the onset and development of true friendship with his children. Having reached the crucial goals of development together, the father must first allow the independence of his children, followed by their return and a review of their progress. Once again life is like a dance with the endless rhythm of goings and comings. The first of these movements away from Dad is likely to be painful because the young adult must find his or her own identity separate from Mom and Dad. The first step is often to declare oneself different than one's parents on some important point. To some parents this appears to be rejection. Daughters want to be women and have their own boyfriends. Sons want to be different in ways that often mean ignoring Dad for a few years in favor of their own friends and interests. If Dad is prone to fear rejection, he will use these cues to withdraw from his children rather than encouraging their development as individuals.

As adult children approach different milestones, they turn to their father for encouragement, then run off and forget him only to return later for his praise, interest, and appreciation of their success. Should, per adventure, their efforts result in failure, their return is likely to be quicker. When faced with his children's failures, Dad gets a chance to relive a little of the "kiss the boo-boo" days before the cycle repeats. Major milestones are first dates, driving the car, getting a job, going to college, getting engaged and then married, buying a car or a house, or even new tires.

I can recall trying to decide whether I should buy steel-belted or radial ply tires and asking my dad to help me choose. The same was true for what car battery was best or what sort of life insurance policy I needed. These sorts of decisions brought me back to Dad long after I was married.

The character of a father-and-child relationship in adulthood becomes increasingly like that of adult peers. As children begin to approach the same point in life at which they can actually remember watching their parents, times of sharing take on a special sweetness. "I remember thinking how old my parents were at thirty-five and now I'm thirty-five," such a parent might say. Adult children are now eager to compare their experiences with what they remember of their parents as well as what they experience. How am I different? How am I like my parents? For parents this fulfills the old prophecy, "You'll understand when you're older," and provided that they let their children make the point, it now cements the bond.

A father is gratified with each renewal of his children's interest in who he is. Each incident allows him renewed opportunity to express how much of his children he has treasured and guarded inside, and how he has blended all the forces that made the child unique.

THE WOUNDED FATHER OF YOUNG MEN AND WOMEN

The father who crashed as he attempted passage into manhood is in for a bumpy ride when his children take the steering wheel. He will find strong impulses to react the way his parents did or precisely the opposite. Since the most common symptom of this problem is a continuation of the reactive identity of early teenage years, this father is usually marked by being reactive and negative towards his children. He may criticize the way his children dress, their choice of friends, their personal styles, or their approach to college and work.

A reactive identity is one where the person defines him- or herself in terms of what he or she is not. It can range from the response, "I'm not stupid, you are," to the complex, "I'm not like my parents and family." It is seen in tastes and choices. Reactive identities know what they don't like or want or value, but not what they do like, want, and value.

The second error common to fathers who experienced trouble during their own coming of age is that they tend towards extremes—that is to say, their own style is reactive. They are either too involved and controlling or too withdrawn and detached. They provoke standoffs and draw lines in the sand, making every move their child makes a challenge to Dad's authority. Even steps towards normal growth become major risks for the child because Dad says, "If you move out, don't expect any help from me!"

Billy had such a father. Billy's dad was an assistant pastor in a large church. Whenever anything went wrong in Billy's life, his dad was quick to point out which transgression caused the trouble. Billy felt he could not do anything without provoking his father's anger. One day at school Billy's best friend was shot to death right in front of him by another kid. The police said it was probably a random gang killing. Billy did not dare to tell his father what had happened, because the boy was already upset enough without having his father yell at him about "hanging" around with the wrong friends again.

Immediately, Billy's grades dropped. He could not concentrate in class and was afraid to go to school. His father was outraged that Billy was not getting good grades and grounded him from everything but church. He yelled at the boy almost every day and even took him to the youth pastor at church to have him correct the boy's "rebellious attitude." Perhaps it will not surprise you that before six months were up, Billy was thinking seriously that his dead friend had it better and was making plans to join him. Nothing would induce the father to spend time with Billy or even take a day away for his son. "When he gets his grades up, we'll talk about it. He is lazy and I won't reward bad behavior." The more his dad reacted, the less Billy wanted to tell him of his pain and loss. As a result, Billy's life hangs in the balance.

Lesser versions of this scenario provide the most common forms of counseling problems with teenagers and young adults. Most fathers who are caught in this trap can't believe it is more about them than about their children because they are trying so hard and really believe they are doing the right thing. Never do they stop to ask if they are satisfied, rather they concern themselves with being justified. Typically, they react against their wife's observations and the feelings of their other children with simply more self-justification. Since they have not become men, they do not seek the correction of other men either, although if they did they might soon grow and turn their hearts back towards their children.

In most cases it is the strength of the father's bond with his children that inspires him to provide for his children the very things he did not receive and feel with them the emotions he was not allowed to experience. In giving this life to his children, the father finds expression for the very best part of himself. This bond is both his connection to the world and his incentive to make the world better.

But what exactly is a father's world like? We explore that question in the next chapter.

ELEVEN

The Father's World

IF INDEED IT IS GOOD TO BE A MAN, not in contrast to being a woman, but just because being what God made one to be is splendidly good, then how rewarding it is to be a father! The father is a source of life to others. Furthermore, every man who does not become a source of life to others will remain unfulfilled and, therefore, miserable. The man who lives to be a consumer will die with the most toys to be fought over by the heirs to his estate. In the end he still must give up his life, but only when he can no longer enjoy doing so. Who can say if anyone but the Internal Revenue Service loves him for it.

Because it so upsets us, we may be tempted to ignore perverted forms of life-giving. The man who gives life only to insure his own supply of pleasure is shocking to us, and rightly so. This is the kind of person who inspires children's stories of witches that fatten you up so they can eat you. Solomon says that it is better to put a knife to your throat than to enjoy the dainty morsels of such a person. The most common version of this horror is the man who acts fatherly and then sexually abuses the children he lures into his grasp. When this is done by fathers to their children or stepchildren, we call it incest. When men fatten up other people's children to eat, we call it pedophilia. Whatever name we use, the revulsion and horror remain because life-giving is not intended as a way to insure the life-giver's supply of pleasure.

Three times in Scripture God tells us, "You shall not boil a kid in its mother's milk" (Ex 23:19; 34:26; Dt 14:21). The milk which gives a kid its life is not to be used to enhance the pleasure of consuming it. There is an important biblical principle at work here that applies to other situations as well. How much more, for instance, are we to keep the natural beauty and sexuality of our children protected from the chance we will use it to enhance our own pleasure! We would be more innocent if we simply cooked our children and ate them as the wicked have done (Dt 28:53-54). Further, while we are not to live in fear, we must take reasonable precautions to protect our children from likely predators or pedophiles.

But some will say, what about the case where the child is not the biological relative of the man? The story of the good Samaritan is well known because it teaches that a neighbor is defined by acting neighborly to everyone he or she meets. Likewise, any man entrusted with the care of children is a father to them whether he likes to think so or not. He will be judged accordingly, with no reduction of standards. The privilege of giving life brings with it the prohibition of consuming the life we give for our own pleasure. If we have been given much, then much will be required of us.

A source of life is never ignored for long, whether it is a spring in the desert or a herd of zebras on the Serengeti Plain, someone is bound to notice. Life springs up around such life-giving places, and demand often brings with it competition.

Although man's basic nature is fatherly, actual examples of fatherliness are sometimes rare. Fathers in such places find high demands placed on them. Even where good fathers are plentiful, there are usually enough needs in the broader community that a father must take more than his own children into consideration.

There is rarely a fair distribution of resources. Frequently a few fathers do the yeoman's share, while other potential fathers do nothing and suffer pangs of emptiness. Perhaps the easiest case to see is the man and wife who have no biological children of their own. Men in this state often feel the calling of fatherhood most acutely. Some, for emotional or economic reasons, decide not to have children and feel that the best way to protect their children is not to bring them into a cruel world. As fathers to phantom children, they feel the empty yearning of protecting without the joy of giving life.

Many couples are childless for other reasons. Rather than list possible reasons, we will focus on the need for everyone to experience giving life. Like the single man who fathers, whom we will study in the next chapter, these fathers must give life to those who need supplementary, stand-in, or replacement fathers. In this way, they help balance the load for other fathers and find fulfillment for themselves.

Supplementary fathers. Every child is in need of supplementary fathers. These are fathers who assist the child's main father with training, introduction into the community, and appreciating parts of the child and the world that the father does not know, or lacks the opportunity to enjoy. My sons have benefitted from supplementary fathers. Wayne Bishop helped my son Jamie rebuild a carburetor, while Chuck Rose took Rami through the Gospel of John. There is always a need for supplementary fathers, even in the best of homes. We should not be misled into believing that supplementary fathers are only needed in childhood. It is a life-long need.

Stand-in fathers. Sometimes, due to illness, death, distance, moral breakdown, or abandonment, a primary father does not provide even minimum requirements for his children. These children require a partial replacement of their father. One young woman may want a favorite uncle to give her away at her wedding after the death of her father, or a young man might want someone to watch him compete since his father left town with another woman. This stand-in father will take the father's place at significant moments in the child's life, like remembering to send a birthday card or coming to the house at Christmas. This is a role akin to that of a foster father or godfather.

Replacement fathers. Faced with a catastrophic loss of a parent through violence, crime, moral delinquency, or disaster, some people face the need of a new father or mother. Legal adoption is needed for young children and its spiritual equivalent for adults. It has been my privilege to observe many replacement fathers since almost all my close friends have adopted children—some from India, others from Mexico, even one from Indiana.

There are many different levels at which it is possible to be a father. Consequently, since there is a large demand for good fathers, men are never at a loss for opportunities. Since people need fathers at all ages, and no one with only one father has enough fathers, let us consider a few possibilities starting with the most controversial situation first.

MAN AS FATHER TO HIS WIFE

Every man will marry a woman who has deficits in her bonds with her father, for there is no father who can entirely avoid putting some glass into his daughter's face. Every woman will marry a man who has deficits in his bonds with his mother, for there is no mother who can completely avoid grinding some glass into her son's face. Healthy couples often address this problem by temporarily serving as supplemental parents for each other. That is to say, when one partner slips into their childhood feelings, the healthy spouse will respond like a good parent should.

Within a healthy marital bond, there is room for both partners to be adults at the same time in order to run a household. Both can then be children at the same time in order to play. And occasionally they can even be parent and child to each other in order to heal and straighten themselves out. At times, it is even permissible for the arrangement to be lopsided with one spouse doing more parenting and the other more feeling and play, provided the arrangement is understood to be temporary.

Not all such situations are short-lived. The clearest case I remember was one I observed as a counselor in a camp for senior citizens. One woman in the camp was an offense to the other campers. She would knock down women with their walkers to get to the front of the food line. She refused to take a shower and was easily recognizable from downwind. She was intensely reactive and hostile if confronted. In all she was most unpleasant.

Her husband was one of the most educated and interesting men I have ever met. Fluent in seventeen languages, he added a wealth of knowledge to any conversation. He was kind, interested in the people around him, and put up with his wife's outrages with saintly patience, all the while redirecting her to better behavior—like a good father would do with a two-year-old.

Disgruntled, I asked him why he put up with a wife who acted so childishly. He told me that she had not always been that way; but only for the last twenty-five years since Auschwitz. A victim of Nazi torture and non-anesthetized surgery on her brain, his wife, who had once been a concert pianist, had been reduced to this state. His stay in the concentration camps had gone better than hers and even increased his understanding of other languages, which is proof that some people can find something good anywhere.

Many older couples find themselves in a similar scenario. But it is entirely different for a couple to face the consequences of illness, accidents, and calamity together than it is to enter a marriage in order to find a parent. Most women who try to marry a father-figure are still at the four-year-old level of emotional development. Four-year-old girls want to marry Daddy and are sure they can take better care of him than Mommy can. However, girls who have not outgrown this stage by the time they marry carry within themselves the jealous rage of childhood. A four-year-old girl wants to be special, the only girl in Daddy's life. She is an attachment vigilante intent to protect her place with Dad. Such behavior is tolerable, even a bit cute, in a four-year-old. But when lodged in an adult body with its knowledge and abilities, jealousy becomes a terror and a horror.

Four-year-old children and their adult counterparts give care based on the hope that in giving they will receive equal care in return. This version of consuming the life one gives leads to an endless succession of upsets as hurt rage follows hurt rage. It makes me think of the time I slipped at the top of a sleet-covered stairway and felt my tender parts hit one step after another all the way to the ground floor.

The man who joins himself to a woman after mistaking her devoted love for Daddy with an adult love for a husband will rue the day he said, "I do." Not only so, but should the woman outgrow this four-year-old stage at some point, she will lose interest in taking care of her man, leaving her ex-husband to feel that she took him in with promises of love and then took him for everything she could.

The man trapped in such an arrangement often buys security by using his life-giving capacity to insure his own source of supply. He will often expect to take care of such a woman in return for having her please him. Since life-giving carries with it the prohibition of consuming the life we give for our own pleasure, such arrangements always backfire. Long-term father-and-daughter relationships are an inadequate model for a marriage relationship.

Still it is often the woman who encourages her husband to become a better father for their children and in so doing receives some vicarious fathering. In addition, since father is the prototypical male in every daughter's life and she understands her femininity primarily in relationship to Dad's masculinity, anything a husband does to change his wife's view of men or her femininity makes him, for that moment, a supplemental father. This is a helpful role and even healing.

A man told me how his wife had hidden one of his shirts which she did not like. When he asked her to return it, she said, "You can beat me if you want, but I won't get it." Raised by an abusive father, she could not appreciate her husband's patience and concern.

"I knew I was speaking for good fathers everywhere," he told me, "when I said, 'I'm not going to hurt you. I just want my shirt.'" Then he gave her a hug. In that moment, he was a supplemental father for his wife. He was a life-giver.

MAN AS A FATHER TO HIS CHILDREN'S FRIENDS

"Enough for us and some to share." This motto should be found in every home. It is a good measure for the amount of love needed to produce satisfaction. Enough for us with some to share is the dosage of attention children need. On open house nights at school, the parents who pay attention to their child's efforts and those of the child's friends or table-mates become popular and spread a blanket of good will for the child to enjoy in school. Even in such places as scouts, baseball leagues, or camps, the parents who pay attention to their children's friends really stand out. Not only so, but the parent who sends along an extra cookie for the child to share, or makes room for one more on the way to the amusement park or church, allows their child to share the best treasure—his parents. Comments like, "Your dad is cool!" or, "Your mom is really nice!" please parent and child alike.

If you look around, you will find parents that almost always have an extra participant in family activities. It is having enough and some to share that produces this effect. Children in such families are provided the means to give good experiences to friends and prove that their dad and mom are the greatest.

Although they are school teachers and not wealthy, Wayne and Judi always found room for some of their children's friends to travel with them to Mexico or Europe. Dean and Diane always made room for Paul's friends on camping and ski trips. Spence and Bonnie fit in kids for high school football games and youth activities. Dick and Nancy always had extra soft drinks when the kids rented a movie.

Willard and Virginia always had cookies on Sunday afternoon for all the kids and their parents who wanted to come over and swim. Hundreds of children learned to swim in their backyard pool. Kids from Africa to Australia look to Willard and Virginia as supplementary parents. While Virginia was the one who seemed to have a way with kids, Willard kept everything safe and operational and provided constant supervision for backyard activities.

I read a true story once of a father who allowed his daughter and her little friend to "fix" his hair and then took them both to a restaurant with his outrageous styling job. This allowed his daughter to share her wonderful dad and approach life with the vision of enough with some to share. What a contrast with the woman who told me that she turned to her childhood friend for support these days because she was the other one her dad liked to make out with.

MEN AS GODFATHERS

In various sacramental traditions, the role of the godfather is a very special one. In Spanish, the word for godfather is "compadre," or literally "co-father." Besides the spiritual responsibility to bring the children up in the ways of the Lord should the father be absent, co-fathers used to provide real-life security for children in a world where illness or war could claim the father's life and leave the child unprotected. Thus fathers saw it as one of their first duties before God to obtain a back-up father who would make a commitment to care for each of their children for life.

Sadly, we all know that many times this can and does become simply an honorary tradition with little content. But the idea of a father and co-father agreeing to the mutual care of a child has many spiritual, social, and personal advantages. Not only does this role provide a way for single men to participate in fathering, it also gives children a sense of a spiritual family which extends beyond their biological ties right from the start.

MAN AS A FATHER TO OTHER MEN

Fathers encourage and comfort each other. Derrick, a young father, recently approached another young father and asked him if he felt neglected too. Derrick's own father had been very controlling and on at least one occasion had an affair in front of his son. Now that Derrick's wife was absorbed with their baby and had been short and cross with him for about a year, he was finding the interest shown by other women alarmingly attractive.

Derrick's friend talked to him about the occasional struggles he felt himself when his wife would say, "The baby comes first." By sharing his feelings and encouraging Derrick to hang in there until he earned the special love of his little daughter, the friend became a supplemental dad. He filled in where Derrick's father's failures had left a gap. He illustrated what a good dad would do.

Much more extensive roles are possible between men, but a discussion of stand-in and replacement fathers for men must wait for the chapters on man as an elder or grandfather.

MAN AS A FATHER AFTER DIVORCE

Single-parent dads. The first and most obvious result of divorce is the presence of two single parents. In addition to the effort of single parenthood, there is lots of emotional pain in everyone's life which brings out hidden problems and drives other problems into hiding.

Under this load, the single parent who is a father must do his best to be both Mom and Dad as we described them in chapters two and three. While this job is impossible, it must be attempted all the same. Not only does this help avoid further polarization of the parents and of gender-specific roles, but children need attention both to what goes in and what comes out of them on a daily basis. This leaves single parents to be both father and mother when they have custody of the children. Since the wise father always finds other fathers (and, in this case, mothers) for his children, he will need to lean more heavily on their help in order to avoid collapse.

Dad and his ex-wife. Some have said that the mother is the main interpreter of the father to her children. Through her eyes, they come to view his time at work as an act of love or a way to stay away from his family. Never is the father more vulnerable to this kind of interpreting than during a divorce and while separated from his children. Wise mothers interpret the father's actions truthfully, not according to their own moods and fears.

The dad who knows himself to be a life-giver will continue to care for his children. He will avoid, as best he can, wasting life and resources in fighting his ex-wife. The major trap for divorcing couples is when both parties react to each other rather than express who they really are. Hurt and trapped feelings lead to rejection and avoidance, rather than Dad acting like the man and father he knows himself to be. Vindictiveness has made more than one father become what his ex-wife said he was, amid shouts of, "Well, if she wants it that way!"

The determination to live according to one's own character should rule in relationship to one's ex-wife. The father must do his best to become the faithful interpreter of his own actions—actions which while loving may not be understandable to children. Children, particularly young children, do everything because it is what they want and like to do. Thus, they will interpret all their parents' actions to mean the same. If Dad or Mom is not with them, it is because the parent does not like to be with them. Parents are always viewed as doing what they like.

To avoid making these childish misunderstandings a permanent part of the child's identity, the wise father will give an interpretation of his and his ex-wife's actions that is realistic. These interpretations will need to be made repeatedly until the child is able to understand a world in which people do not always do what they like to do.

In all, the goal is to give life to children so if they cannot have one home in which they grow up loved and wanted, they have two homes in which to grow up loved and wanted.

Dad as stepfather. Divorces tend to happen because people's ability to love is exceeded by the force of their feelings. In other words, people divorce because their feelings change. The most common explanation given to children about divorce is, "Your parents don't love each other any more." This makes for a terrifying situation for children, who can then never be sure when love will run out for them as well. In addition, they learn that who one loves is not a matter of choice but of what one feels. This lesson is clearly applied to the relationship to stepfathers. Since Mom did not love Dad, just because he was Dad, neither will the child love Stepdad just because he is Stepdad. Stepparents, therefore, often inherit the storm of feelings that the child now believes are the rule of life. The rule goes something like this: If I love you fine, but, if I don't, then any treatment or rejection is justified. Most children of divorce are left with an internal rule similar to this. It is the bane of blended families.

Stepfathers may experience a slow progression from being a supplemental father to being a replacement father. In other cases, which usually involve younger children, men may find themselves suddenly thrust into the father role with no time for adjustment. Men find it quite painful when their father love is rejected by their new wards. The man who has not learned the value of love that suffers will withdraw or become controlling and angry. He ceases to love as a dad and becomes the boss.

At the other extreme is the stepfather who, rather than giving life as a father would, consumes it for his pleasure. His attraction to the children is more likely to become sexual since he has not gone through the process of cleaning dirty diapers, getting spit up on, staying up nights, cleaning snot from a filthy face, or getting a finger up his nose. For it is all those irritating moments of closeness that help most fathers develop a nonsexual touch and love for their children.

The man who knows his feelings, his needs, and what will bring him satisfaction will find stepparenting to be a satisfying expression of his ability to give life when he realizes that he has nothing to prove. He is a dad and his job is finding ways to express the best of himself. If his audience appreciates him, that's fine; if they do not, then his character will shine even brighter for he is still a dad whether anyone appreciates it or not. Children do not make one a dad, they only provide the opportunity to express it.

THE FATHER AND HIS WORK

No chapter on being a dad would be complete without mentioning Dad's work. Most dads find their work to be both the most continuous part of fatherhood and the thing that most prevents them from being the dad they want to be. One friend of mine said that a book on being a dad need contain only one page—a picture of a man taking out his billfold. One woman said that the difference between a father's relationship with his daughter and his son is that the son wants the keys to the car and the daughter wants the credit card. Credit card, car keys, and billfold all depend on a man's work. Yet it is work that keeps Dad from the track meet after school, the violin recital (thankfully), and the class play. Work puts Dad in a bad mood by the time he gets home and drains the best of his energy before he can make good on his promise to play ball in the park.

Unlike Matthew, in the John Denver song by the same title, who "rode on his daddy's shoulders, behind a mule, beneath the sun," most American boys and girls do not work with their dads. Some, like the children in *Mary Poppins*, venture into their father's workplace almost in wonder or even fear.

To a man, his work is his life poured out minute by minute and returned to him in an envelope every two weeks. When the government, unions, insurance companies, and other parasites have taken their share, all but the most wretched of men will take what is left of their earnings home to keep their family alive. It might not seem like much, and in spite of all the quips about "bringing home the paycheck," this too is life-giving.

A man who knows he is a good thing and can give away the life he has received will have many opportunities to do so. He must be strong or his life will be stolen before he can give it away, and he must know who he is or he will be shaped into whatever pleases the consumers around him. This life-giving ability is the main event in men's lives. In the next chapter we will see how men who have not become fathers biologically express this life.

TWELVE

Single and Childless
Men as Fathers

I WANT MEN TO KNOW that they have something of great value to give to children. Men are to be the source of life to others. Men have something of great value to give because God has created them with the ability to see other people as they were meant to be. A father is one who helps his children find their true identity in spite of cultural distortions and his own injuries. There is nothing about getting married or starting a pregnancy that automatically makes a man better able to see others with the eyes of God.

Some single men may have skipped to this chapter and bypassed the chapters on men as fathers to children and the father's world. Take time to go back and read them even if it seems uncomfortable, or even painful. Many single men feel resistance inside towards reading about children. This probably comes from distorted beliefs that culture and family have programmed into male identities. Men are meant to be dads.

It was the prayer of my teenage years that God would let me see Jesus in others. When I looked at a girl and said, "Now, where do I see Jesus in her?" it had an influence on how I treated her. To this day, seeing Jesus in a boy changes my attitude towards him. My teenage prayer was the beginning of a gift. God began giving me the eyes of heaven through which people appeared quite changed. The driver who gave me the finger and honked his horn became blind and small rather than large and threatening. Girls without bras became lonely and needy instead of being the keepers of the great treasure. Seeing people as God would see them helped me act accordingly. I now had a gift to give anyone who would receive it, for really seeing into someone's heart is perhaps the greatest gift a man can give. Fathers give this gift when they help others to see themselves correctly.

Julie had very few friends. Almost everyone told her she was terrible. It wasn't uncommon for people to say rather insulting and vulgar things to her which she answered in kind. "Everyone hates me," she told her pastor, who was also her replacement father. "Everyone hates me, except for you. You keep telling me that I'm a blessing. Why do you tell me that I'm a blessing?"

"Because that is what God created you to be," said her pastor. "It is a father's job to tell you the truth about yourself for a change. I know I'm up against an awful bunch of liars who have told you that you were created to be something else, but that isn't the truth about you. You were created to be a blessing, and anything other than that is a lie."

The same thing is true for every man. Every man was created as a blessing. It is the only reason God would have created you. He was not interested in creating his people as curses, but as blessings. That is what he put in your father before you and now in you. Your father may not have followed God's design, but the father within every man is meant as a blessing to his children.

Julie's father had put other things in her heart. Every time she got angry her father would say, "Whats-a-matter, you need to get laid?" Little wonder that in time her first reaction when provoked was a two-word phrase ending in "you!"

When we see the image of God in others, we begin giving life and form to them. The desire to do so comes from the father's heart in each man. Single men and married men without children are capable of this type of life-giving and will be unfulfilled without it.

God established men as protectors and nurturers of his garden. That is what it means to be a man. Men protect and make things grow. That is why it is good news to have men around. This is the basis of fatherhood. Yet if the man's own history has not been redeemed by God, he will have nothing redeemable to offer to others. Without knowing our own redemption, we cannot see others through the eyes of heaven and so bring them life. When we only see garbage in others, we will not know who they were created to be.

Men with the eyes of heaven and a redeemed history are certainly ready to be fathers. This life-giving strength is to be given away, whether it is to our extended families or our spiritual families. The man who offers such gifts to others is being a father whether he is married, has children, or is single.

A case can certainly be made that if one wishes to be a father it is better to remain single and celibate. Marriages are demanding of time, energy, and resources. First Corinthians, chapter seven contains a classic and controversial discussion on this topic that has led many to conclude that Paul was against marriage. In this passage, Paul says that it is better not to marry unless sexual passions get too strong. Many have concluded that Paul thought Christians should stay single, if they can.

This understanding of the passage is based on reading verse 26, which speaks of "a time of stress like the present," and verse 29, which says, "The time we live in will not last long," in referring to the ongoing life of the church. I believe the passage refers to times of extreme stress. Paul was writing to a church under violent, horrifying persecution.

Having lived through times of persecution when Christians were driven from their homes in the middle of the night and forced to escape with their wives and children, I find Paul's description to be true. The missions context in which I grew up in Colombia was exceedingly violent at times. When fleeing for his life, a married man is not thinking of the Lord's children, he is thinking about his wife and kids and how to find them food and shelter. It is, as Paul describes, a bad time to marry and raise a family. Staying single does save grief and pain, if one can handle it, until the brief time of trouble is over. Those who have seen their children tortured or starved to death will witness the truth of this statement.

The single person, on the other hand, can and does devote time to the care of others during times of extreme stress. In that sense the single person can be a supplemental, stand-in, or replacement father, a brother or a friend to more people than a married man can. Pastors and missionaries who plan to go into high-stress locations should listen to Paul's excellent instruction and stay out if they are married with children. In any case, Paul is clear that the single person can care for more children than the married person if he or she is devoted to Christ.

Under normal conditions, marriages do form the most desirable way of having children because they are the most uniform and disciplined way of providing care for a family. The non-stop effort afforded by a lifetime commitment to one's child produces character which cannot be duplicated by any other method. The parent who throughout life sustains a child's life and growth develops a breadth of love that covers all things. The single person who, in times of severe stress, loves many children and endures the deaths of many children builds a depth of love that cannot be duplicated either. Both loves are strong because they flow from the person's life itself—life which in turn flows from God.

We should not go on, however, to assume that single men are only meant to parent children in times of stress. True, they are most helpful at such times, but the call for single men to become fathers goes far beyond stressful periods in history to stressful times in everyday life. Every child needs more dads. Most single men don't notice the opportunities because they have hidden their desire to become fathers.

The central message for single men is that if they do not know having children is satisfying, they will not desire children.

Men who do not desire children will not have any and so their ignorance seals their fate. Men who look inside themselves will find something pulling them towards children—something pushing them to be a source of life. This force is alive and is strong within them. Some will recognize it for what it is, the call to be a father.

THE UNWEANED CHILD

There are actually many places for a single man to experience fatherhood. It is hardest for single men to become fathers to unweaned children. Few opportunities are afforded except within the extended family context. Single men do find opportunities to become father figures to extended family members. This is the most natural place to experience the long-term commitment of fatherhood. No child with only one father has enough fathers; nieces, nephews, and younger cousins can all provide opportunities. Naturally, if the child has no father, his or her need will be greater, but it is not necessary to find an extremely needy child in order to experience fatherhood.

THE WEANED CHILD

All fathers are life-givers. The single man should express the life that lies within himself whether it comes out through cooking, hiking, art, music, sports, working, exploring, or simply talking. This is the life he has to offer to children. The weaned child is beginning to explore life and seek satisfaction. He needs the life that the single man finds within himself. It is a simple matter to share what one loves with children by simply including them. Of course, this assumes that the single man can locate a child with which to share his life.

After exhausting possibilities within his extended family, the man may seek children within organizations in his community or through his church. As with biological fathers, such single men should seek more than one father for their children. An isolated father is always in trouble, and single men should not think that they have been granted an exemption to this rule. Parents should be warned not to share their children with fathers or mothers who live and act alone; trouble will usually come of it. By living alone, I do not mean people who live by themselves in their own house or apartment, but those whose practice of parenting is solitary whether they live with others or not.

The involvement of single men fits in well with the father's task in caring for the weaned child. The father introduces the child to the community and teaches him or her satisfaction. Dad must rely on his own knowledge of satisfaction, but the final test is always the child's own experience.

Becoming a father to weaned children is far easier for most single men. Not only are there opportunities like children's clubs, Sunday schools, and group sporting events, but many single men can be fathers in junior high ministries, perhaps through their church. Junior high is the time that many children experience their first conscious rejection by their fathers. Fathers often react to their children by rejecting their independence at a time when children are still very concerned about their parents' attention. In many churches, camps, and activity centers, this parenting gap is filled by young would-be fathers.

Sports is another arena where single men tend to congregate. Older brothers, single uncles, and occasional sports enthusiasts become supplemental fathers to young players learning the ropes. Most single men stay at the supplemental-father stage. Occasionally, an uncle will become a stand-in father for his nephews and nieces, particularly following a divorce or a father's death.

YOUNG ADULTS

Single men also have a wonderful opportunity to be fathers when boys go through their rite of passage into manhood. Just as the men in Dan's church surrounded each boy, teaching him about life and making a commitment to follow up their teaching with opportunities to practice, single men have as much to teach boys about history and manhood as married fathers do. Single men often have more time available, so their contribution can be greater. If a group of single men took on the rites of passage for the boys of their community, they would have enough sons to last the rest of their lives.

Fathers are needed even as children become adults. Young men and women often need someone to help them when conflicts escalate excessively at home. Occasionally, a single man will even become a replacement father through adoption or foster parenting. One pastor I know, although he never married, took in a boy and a girl who were abandoned on the street as teenagers. These new charges lived with him until they were adults. He paid for the girl's wedding and helped the boy buy a car. He became, in all important respects, their father for life.

BECOMING A GOOD FATHER

To fully experience fatherhood, the single man must take time to consider what he is doing. Fathers need to take time to think about being fathers. Fathers must ask themselves, "What would a father do in this or that situation?" The single man may be misled into thinking that his lack of ideas on how to be a successful father comes from his lack of biological children, but such is not the case. Even with biological children, fathers learn to act like fathers by asking themselves, their friends, and family, "What would a father do now?"

After some planning the father must test his idea to see if it works. The efforts that are generated by careful planning are then judged to see if they are satisfying, so each new attempt is refined. This discipline brings out more of what is best in the father.

Many men find that their first answers to the question about what a father would do brings to mind answers that require punishment. After all, many people's conscious thoughts about fathers have never been stretched beyond spanking, grounding, or shouting. By this point in the book, we do not need to combat those notions, rather we should encourage each fledgling father or single man to seek the things that make him feel he is giving life to children in his care.

I remember one of my first fathering experiences was as a camp counselor. Teamed with another young single man, I took on the little "rowdies" in a daily challenge to see who would tire the other out first. Believing ourselves to be strong and firm counselors, we were proud of our cabin. We thought of ourselves more as camp counselors than as fathers at the time. Pleased with our management of the boys, we would brag about our cabin to the other counselors.

Several of the women counselors insisted that the boys were afraid of us. We did not believe it. "Ask them," said the women, so we did. The boys reported that they were afraid which made us rethink our whole approach. This kind of learning was possible only by living in a wider community. All good fathers will combine what they learn from their community with the internal test of satisfaction to insure that what purports to be good biblical advice really works and is solid.

A final note. I do not believe that in practice there should be a separation of married fathers and single men who father. What is needed by both types of fathers is the strength and experience of their elders, the truly *Grand Fathers* of the community. It is grandfathers who help men become fathers—just as fathers help boys become men. So let us now move on to the grandfathers or elders.

THIRTEEN

Becoming an Elder

THE FIRST HOUSE I BOUGHT belonged to Walter Gilbert, a school teacher. The house itself was designed in part by his daughter since he involved her in building the house. The back of the house has what Walter called a "mother-in-law apartment." There his mother-in-law, and after her, many other people found shelter. When he retired, Walter took his elder status seriously and helped his pastor with most of those who came to the church for help. Walter took care of others in need. One neighbor bought his plot of land from Walter when he arrived in the United States, fleeing the Holocaust and war in his land. To this day he tells stories about the kindness and fairness of "Mr. Walter."

Our houses, cities, churches, and lives are full of history. We are heirs to rich traditions of elders—their stories quietly lived out around us. Somewhere along the way many of us have forgotten to investigate our roots, so our elders are quietly passing away, leaving a generation who believe that relevance means new data.

However, data will become obsolete. Pages of statistical analysis from my dissertation hardly interest the paper recyclers these days. Yet, we madly pursue the new, assuming that all old information is no more important than my dissertation now is. In learning how to get our computer mice through windows and twice as much data on our hard disks, we are forgetting to back up our working environment. It is analogous to the way we too easily forget the treasures found only in the minds of the elders.

When I first learned to program a computer, we used little cards with holes punched into them to make statements telling the computer what to do. Certain words were "reserved" by the computer for use as commands, while other words could be defined by the programmer. Like computers, people have reserved words as well, words that have special meanings to insiders. To Latin Americans "Jesus" might be any kid's name like Tom or Bob, but to English speakers "Jesus" refers to the Christ. His name is a "reserved word" to one group and not another.

When I first bought a car, I went down to the auto parts store and asked for some gunk to clean my car. But in auto parts stores Gunk is a brand name—a "reserved word"—and does not mean "just any sort of stuff" to clean cars. As a result, I ended up in the engine cleaning department instead of the car washing section. I had used a reserved word by mistake.

THE FOURTH STAGE—BECOMING AN ELDER

Elder is a word with reserved meanings for some groups; and yet, because it more closely describes the fourth stage of manhood, we will use "elder" rather than grandfather, mentor, or "old goat" to refer to this stage.[1] An elder, as we will define the term, is a man who has raised children to be adult men and women and is ready to be a father to others outside his immediate family. Age does not make an elder, biological grandchildren do not make an elder, having children outside your own home does not make an elder, it is the readiness to treat others in your community as you have treated your own family that makes a man an elder.

It is understood in many tribal societies that ruling is left to elders. These elders maintain the history and culture of their people. In India men are expected to reach a point in their life where their concerns expand beyond their own house to include their village. This is another expression of the elder's role in a traditional society. The home is the training ground for the elder, who having practiced on those born to him, can now be trusted with the lives of those he did not engender. Elders rule, guard, teach, and oversee. In this way they are fathers to their people, their city, the stranger, and the orphan.

Octavio Paz said of the macho man, "He is not of our city." The macho man is the antithesis of the elder because he measures his masculinity by death and consumption, not by preserving and giving life. When a macho view of life is used by elders as a way to protect tradition and their own village, the results are violent and oppressive as described by Hugh Steven in his book, *They Dared to Be Different*. Steven describes the social and spiritual changes which followed the translation of the Bible for the Chamula people of Mexico. The Chamula elders have a view of masculinity very similar to that described by Paz. Chamulas have a saying, "To deviate is to die." Chamula elders are the keepers of their tradition, an abusive and alcoholic tradition. Those who will not consume the sacred alcohol with them, they kill.

King David, on the other hand, was an elder in a life-giving tradition, although he himself was a man of war. When his city was raided and all the women, children, and riches were carried off, David went after the raiders with his army and got everyone and everything back. The real evidence of his elder capacity came when he returned. David insisted that the recovered goods be shared between those who went to battle and those who stayed and stood guard. He looked out for all the members of his community.

Elders become elders, rather than tyrants, by going through the first three stages of life. You will recall that each stage builds on the previous one rather than replacing it. An elder has gone through the process of becoming a child many times—once with each child he raised, in addition to his own childhood. This equips him with refined and mature knowledge of his needs, feelings, and sources of satisfaction. He will have introduced each child to the community and helped the child explore and understand his or her world. He will have found elders to be supplemental fathers for his own children and learned from other fathers to teach each child his or her place in the family history.

All of the elder's own children will have become men or women—that is to say, they will be over twelve years old. Only then will a man be ready to consider becoming an elder. He will have trained and will be training his children to treat others fairly and drive a hard yet fair bargain. This kind of experience will have allowed the man approaching the status of elder to understand the needs, feelings, and the required satisfaction of many people within his community. He will also be aware of the dangers his community contains since he has worked for years to protect his children's efforts.

The apostle Paul uses many of these characteristics in his description of elders to Timothy and Titus (1 Tm 3:1-7; Ti 1:6-9). An elder should have his home, his beliefs, and himself in good order. At home an elder should have one wife and orderly children. His home should overflow with hospitality, such that his ties to his community are strong and intact and his reputation is a good one. The elder's own life should be orderly. He cannot be violent, greedy, an alcoholic, envious, self-centered, or easily angered. Instead he must be a good teacher, just, holy, level-headed, faithful, and a friend to good men and women.

In his doctrine, the elder must know God and God's view of people. He faithfully sees others through the eyes of heaven. Thus, he is able to exercise a spiritual fatherhood for those in his care.

It is apparent from even a cursory examination of these characteristics that an elder is well at home with his needs and feelings, able to satisfy himself and others, well practiced in fairness, an experienced father, one who gives love, one who suffers without growing angry or resentful. The elder is a boy, a man, and a father with a wealth of goodness to share.

There is no shortcut to maturity. Becoming an elder requires a high degree of mastery of each one of the preceding stages. The rewards for elders are great. Elders are rewarded with many children. The better an elder is, the more children he will receive. Elders often receive a double inheritance for their endurance since they father both biological and spiritual children.

The passage into the status of elder often arrives through the marriage of a man's children. Fathers adopt additional children when their own children marry. Sons-in-law and daughters-in-law increase the children a man has. In his song "Somewhere in the World," [2] Wayne Watson tells of his prayers for the little girl that will someday grow up to be the wife of his little boy. In-laws become supplemental parents to their new children and clearly herald the onset of elder status.

Fathers who have long taken interest in their children's friends, dates, and loves have anticipated the day of adoption eagerly. In giving away their children to others, they receive children in return, and how great that joy can be. Being welcomed into an accepting and loving family is wonderful for brides and grooms. How hurtful it is when the parents are not inclined to be elders and are judgmental or rejecting. Fathers and elders know that their love has children as its reward. Weddings celebrate this adoption which is why last names have traditionally been changed at weddings.

A further step towards elder status occurs with the arrival of grandchildren. The joy that first-time grandparents show is almost too much for their neighbors at times. Yet these are the rewards of many years of life-giving. A grandfather is the most common expression of elder status. Grandfathers take an interest in all their children's children. Most children love to visit their grandparents. They find there a source of love that is certainly less prone to anger and more leisurely about time than their parents who are so busy. Grandparents are often the saving hope of first-born grandchildren whose parents are so intent on doing things right that they forget to notice their child. Grandparents can take the time to appreciate a child's uniqueness and special gifts.

Loving one's grandchildren is something we often take for granted and view as an extension of the biological family. We expect that a grandfather will love his grandchildren just because they are his. Yet this is itself an expression of love that the grandfather will bestow on someone whom he does not yet know at all. This bond is a father bond to a child he did not father. That is what is meant by extending family bonds, that is what an elder does.

The biological family is not the only inheritance of the elder. Their second inheritance comes in the form of a spiritual family. A spiritual family produces additional children to those who are not barren spiritually. A spiritual parent, or a father to others in the community if you wish, is ready to form paternal bonds with children that are not biologically his own. In addition, elders adopt men to form them as fathers, just as fathers adopt boys to form them as men. When elder men adopt women, it is to make them daughters. In turn, the adoption by elder women is what helps women become mothers and wives.

An elder becomes a father to the mothers and fathers in the community of faith. Just as grandfathers become life-givers to their own biological grandchildren, an elder pours life into the grandchildren that the Lord gives him through his spiritual children, becoming a sort of spiritual grandfather. So he continues to widen his tent pegs as his family grows.

THE STORY OF AN ELDER

But how does an elder get started? Perhaps it would be of interest to know how I came to be an elder. Well, sonny, come here and let me tell you. Just as is true of all the other stages of my life, I stumbled into it. It happened gradually, without my really noticing the change.

It started about the time my sons had both become men. Having two men for sons made me think again how being a man is a good thing. Years of being a father had their effect, making me think and act as a father would—simply because I was one. Being a father touched all areas of my life because it brought out the very best in me.

As a counselor, I felt a father's grief over the ruined lives I saw. People who had started out as beautiful babies had been ravaged by abuse and neglect. One day over lunch with Cathy, a therapist friend of mine, I made a discovery that would forever change the way I thought. A few days later I wrote the following statement.

It seems strange to have children whose bodies are twice as old as mine. My children have been abandoned on doorsteps; neglected; beaten with two-by-fours; shot; sadistically tortured; burned with pokers; raped; molested; betrayed; they have watched as their parents were murdered by terrorists or have even killed each other; they have lost brothers, sisters, mothers, fathers; been sent away to boarding schools at five years of age only to be sent back again and again for years; had parents try to murder them; been chained to tables; locked in closets; suffered in silence for years with guilt, loneliness, disease, paralysis; and at least one killed herself. Their husbands and wives cheat on them. They fight over and play mean tricks on their children, and get divorced....

While all of this happens I have to sit helplessly in my chair and listen, watching as often their bodies and finally their souls become destroyed and lost. Their bodies somehow live on, but the children inside are dead and gone.

There is something wrong with listing griefs this way! Each of these hurts represents someone's life. Children are not comprised of some vast pile of injuries. Each one is a separate individual. After a while I come to know each one, the moods, the defenses, the story.

Sometimes they say, "How can you go from one person to another? Don't you get us confused?" Yes, I am often confused, that comes easily to me, but I know them each right away. Fathers get names wrong sometimes. My dad is forever calling me by my brother's name, but he has never confused the two of us.

A feeling seemed to start for me when my biological son Rami fell out of the second story window onto his head. I think I slowed the car perceptibly for stop signs on the way to the hospital. I noticed the feeling then. It came back when he fell off the ladder and cut his hand so badly, and the time I saw his brother's crushed fingers and injured eye.

When Rami's little friend got his finger caught in the door and it bled all over the playground, Rami said, "My back feels funny, and I get weak in my knees when I think about it. My stomach feels empty. I don't like that feeling!"

That is the feeling! I had it as a boy too, and it didn't go away when I got big, it just has a bigger body on which to play. The pain for others' hurts can be great. Once it was said to Mary, the pain is like "a sword [which] will pierce your own soul too."

Recently, I told my friend in a general way about some of the things which I have recounted here. She said, "You can stop now!" and squirmed uncomfortably. Then she said, "It would make me furious if anyone tried to do those things to my children!" She couldn't say "did those things" only "tried to do those things." The thought could not be imagined. It was then I knew *these are my children*. I cried a lot the next two days.

Many of my children can't bear to remember their lives, and large parts of their memories are a blank. Some don't even know that their souls are lost (to borrow an expression from Dallas Willard) as they work relentlessly to obtain everything they can from life. Perhaps they are the most tragic—the lost who don't even know it!

Am I becoming a partaker in Christ's suffering? Giving up the distance I crave from people and enduring loss hurts me. Those I try to help leave and I never hear from them again. It is like having children who never write (not that they should in this case). Often they won't call even when they desperately need to talk. They don't want to bother me. "It won't make any difference," they say, "You don't care, anyway, it is just your job."

Well, it is my job. But if I had it my way, I'd rather be helping people as a pathologist—stick them with a needle and examine a slide—quite painless to me anyway. Do I get these hours back to add onto the end of my life because "it was just my job"? My job hurts! Sometimes an hour of torture long ago takes years to relive, agony by agony, before the healing will come.

Don't nominate me for sainthood. If there were a way out, I would take it. I know how pathetic my caring really is, how quickly I retreat to safety, how I hate phone calls at home.

It is so hard to care about the insensitive, hostile, belligerent, uncooperative, lying, faithless, irresponsible, dull, uninsightful, moody, untalkative, unresponsive, mean, and hurtful children who can no longer manage to "be nice." And how do I love (dare I use that word?) my arrogant, powerful, controlling, victimizing, over-responsible, rescuing, "got it together," "I'm fine," or terminally nice Christian kids?

Why should I reject them? Every one of those words describes me and God hasn't dumped me. To the contrary, although I am afraid of him, he loves me so much that sometimes it just burns inside.

Will my biological children be jealous that they are not my only children? Do they know that they also have more than the four grandparents they know? For instance, take away "Papa" Walter Trobisch and they are as unlikely to have been born as if one of their genetic grandparents had never been. Yet, I only had fifteen minutes with him in person. Later I read all his books and wrote him a letter. He was the only one who, as I remember, encouraged me to go to graduate school. Not that anyone discouraged me, but only he said "go—do." My other children are in his lineage also.

Will my parents be hurt that I have other parents? Perhaps. Yet they have many other children as well. Now in their seventies they continue to have children. I don't begrudge them. After all, it is caring which is hoarded that withers away. Give liberally and it grows. My life has had hurts, but I have also been healed.

There was a time when I thought I could never even feel angry. Now I bear the exquisite suffering of watching my children tortured before my mental eyes, while I often can't even reach out to touch or hold them. The gift of touch has been so abused that it can no longer heal my daughters. I dare not say, "I care," for that has also been abused. My caring seems so pitifully small anyway—I can't take them all home.

I must even be careful about letting my children know it hurts to see their suffering since some would then try to protect me from it. It would break my heart to see their burden increased. There is no comfort for anyone in trying to be a rock.

Many of my children have suffered attacks, rapes, and incest at the hands of men, fathers, ministers, and psychologists—I am all four. Mothers, fires, terrorists, war, drugs, work, schools, teachers, police, lawyers, and others have all taken their toll. Destruction can come in a moment from any source, and I must watch and listen to the screams, the rage, and finally the silence. This silence is the worst of all, for it speaks of an evil which is unspeakable.

Yet I am above all a child of God—my heavenly Father sustains me. And I must be healed lest the bruised reed be broken. I have cried a lot recently. The ancient and modern masters of torture have known that to torment someone's children can be more painful than to hurt the person him- or herself. Not that my suffering is to be compared to what these little ones have suffered. Yet when I suffer with them, they are healed. "My children" are all his children, and he loved them and knew them before they could say "Father."

God, you know their suffering better than I, for Jesus said, "As you did it to one of the least of these my brethren, you did it to me" (Mt 25:40). I only feel my own pain of having my children suffer; you personally felt everything done to them, even the hurts that they cannot remember. Each day I must entrust my soul, with theirs, to you for life. Often I do not trust you as I should, but there is no one else who can bring the dead to life. Many are the dry and desolate expanses which once were a child full of life and promise.

As I wait in my office to meet a new client, I realize that there may be another child of mine I've never met sitting in the waiting room. Will he or she let me in? Or run from the pain?

So it was that I began to recognize that I was becoming an elder, a limited sort of father to those who needed one. In my relationships with others, I discovered what it meant to be a supplemental father. Indeed, all pastors and counselors become supplemental parents in their work, but for me it didn't stop there.

Strange as it may seem, other counselors, friends, and people at church began to look to me as a father figure. Often it would happen quite innocently. One friend bought a new car—his first new car. He even picked out the stereo system he wanted installed. I was excited for him and asked him to take me for a ride. What a blast we had together. Later he told me that he had always wanted his father to take an interest in his life like I had. He felt that, in a way, he had received that gift from me. What a simple gift to give.

Being a supplemental dad was not the end of the story. Some people needed more, like Renée. Renée is a wonderful young woman whom I have known for a number of years. Her father died some years ago. She has often talked to me about jobs, cars, boyfriends, money, and other things people like to talk over with someone older. One day she brought this nice young man to meet me, and before you know it she was asking me to stand up with her at her wedding and give the father's blessing. I had become a stand-in father in her life. What a joy to watch her walk down the chapel aisle.

In time, I became a stand-in father for Mary Elizabeth also. It started when she had to go to court, then sell her home, buy a car, change careers, and learn how to operate computers. With Mary Elizabeth I learned the importance of a father's role in introducing children to the community, helping them form friendships and find support. In turn, Mary Elizabeth taught me about art, rare foods, the music of John Michael Talbot, Catholic boys, and the Mass. Things did not always go smoothly, as both my family and community did not adapt well to our relationship. In time, and through much pain, we came to be more like brother and sister.

Rick was the first of my spiritual children to arrive as a father himself. With him, I experienced the elder's role in helping men become fathers. The quality of Rick's role models for fathering had truly been abysmal—even criminal. He needed help with almost every area of being a father, except for the desire to be a good dad. This he had in profusion.

Being an elder was immensely satisfying to me, but it took a real push from God to get me over my resistance to becoming a replacement father. Yet a replacement father was just what Eileen needed. I shopped everywhere to find her one, not because I wouldn't want to be a replacement dad, but because I felt myself unsuited for the job. I had had no experience raising daughters; I had only raised sons.

As I resisted, changes took place. Over the span of several years I was given eyes to see Eileen as she really was inside, and then watched as she slowly became what I had seen. A fatherly love for her as a daughter grew so that one day I was ready to hear God's voice say, "Eileen is your daughter."

"But, Lord," I replied, "fathers are life-givers to their children, and I have not given her life."

I was at a soccer game watching my younger son Rami play and not at all expecting a conversation with God. Since I had been studying fatherhood for years, I was even more surprised by what I heard. I could have accepted, "You are like a father," or "You substitute for her father," but to hear such a categorical statement of replacement convinced me I must have heard wrong.

"You have given her life," came the answer. With it I remembered Eileen's words, "I wouldn't be alive today except for you," words I had never wanted to take seriously.

So you see I'm now a proud dad—again. My daughter likes to keep my house full of children she brings home from school. She makes sure I exercise and keep fit because she doesn't want to lose me yet. She dislikes my spending so much time writing, and points out when I mismatch my shirts with my pants. Like all kids, she keeps a careful eye on what I do to be sure I practice what I preach, because she always wants to be able to look up to her dad.

But what of the elder and his relationships with his sons? How does this relationship typically develop, and how does it make a real difference in the lives of men who suffer from father hunger? We'll examine this relationship in chapter fourteen.

FOURTEEN

The Elder and His Sons

THE MEN'S MOVEMENT HAS DRAWN much of its strength from allowing men to admit they need both their fathers and each other. They have adopted the term "mentor" to mean an elder who takes a fatherly interest in a younger man. Although it appears that many men's groups are comprised largely of peers and actual examples of mentors are not the norm, elders are at least being recognized as necessary.

Elders can become supplemental, stand-in, or replacement fathers to other men as the need demands. Such mentor arrangements have led to lifelong commitments between men. Scripture mentions quite a few relationships of this sort. Adoption is frequently mentioned in the Epistles. Little wonder that one of Jesus' last acts on the cross was to perform an adoption ceremony between his elderly mother and her new adult son, John. John became a replacement son for Mary before her first son died. Thus Jesus highlighted the theme of adoption in a prominent way for his followers.

The apostle Paul develops a theology of adoption in Romans 8:15, 23; 9:4; Galatians 4:5; and Ephesians 1:5. In these passages he highlights the believers' new relationship with God. Even if they were once sinners or even non-Jews, they are now adopted children of God. Still, it is his personal practice of adopting other men that illustrates his belief in the family of

God most clearly. If God adopted us, Paul was ready to adopt others as well. Adoption was an expected experience for Paul and other early church leaders.

One example of adoption can be found in the letter Paul wrote on behalf of Onesimus, whom he called "my son... who became my son while I was in chains" (Phlm 10). It is interesting to note that in dealing with Philemon, the Christian who owned the slave Onesimus, Paul addresses him at three levels of development. Since Philemon is not a boy, Paul begins at the level of a man—perhaps Philemon wishes to drive a fair and hard bargain. Paul tells him that if Onesimus owes him anything he, Paul, will pay what is due. In the interest of fairness, Paul further points out that Philemon owes his life to Paul.

Moving on to the level of a father, Paul encourages Philemon to give without receiving in return. Paul points out that Philemon and Onesimus are now in the same eternal family. Then, with a mention of his upcoming visit to Philemon's house, Paul gives him a nudge towards being hospitable and generous and assuming the role of an elder. In this open way, Paul is willing to meet Philemon at whatever level of development he may have reached.

Paul clearly was pleased to have a son, and Onesimus was not his only son. In writing to Titus, Paul greets him as "Titus, my true son in our common faith" (Ti 1:4). In the same way he calls Timothy both "my true son in the faith" (1 Tm 1:2) and his "dear son" (2 Tm 1:2).

Paul is not alone in this practice. His dear brother the apostle Peter refers to Mark as his son in 1 Peter 5:13. They traveled together and Mark interpreted for the old fisherman. Mark probably wrote his Gospel as a traveling companion and catechist for Peter—at least such was the tradition in the early church. In the same way, Paul said of Timothy "as a son with his father he has served with me in the work of the gospel" (Phil 2:22). Adoption and mentoring are intricately combined in these biblical models.

THE PRACTICE OF ELDERS CONTINUES

Christian men continue to put in practice these basic relationships between elders and younger men. George is a divorced contractor in his late fifties. George works hard and plays hard and tries to live a life of integrity. That is not what one expects in a contractor. Ten years ago George took in two men in their twenties whose lives were a mess. They had neither the skills nor the energy to manage their lives successfully. Living with George and working in his company has helped one get off drugs. Both have learned trades, skills, and money and time management. They have learned to live with other people and to work as well as play. George has become the father that neither boy ever had.

Mr. Hansen was a tough old Norwegian. He lived in the north woods, cut his own firewood, built his own buildings, made his own roads, and probably even cut his own hair. Mr. Hansen could pastor a church, teach a class, and sing a song with a conviction that was gripping. When he took young men under his care, they started out splitting wood or grading a road with a rake. They drank stout coffee, ate robust foods, and prayed to God as though he were right there in the woods with them.

Gruff, direct, a man of few words and hard work, Mr. Hansen thought of each boy as his responsibility. He was responsible to see that the boy became a man. He was responsible to see each man became a father. He was responsible to see each father became an elder. And he thought nothing of it. To Mr. Hansen these were the responsibilities of every elder, and he was not one bit unique. His temper flared if boys did not work hard and learn their lessons, so he chose those who worked and discarded those that wouldn't. It was his way—the way of the north-woods elder.

I am glad I knew Mr. Hansen. His driveway was long and full of holes each spring. His woodpile needed careful stacking. I found the work itself was no worse than my previous job in the granite quarries of North Carolina, but Mr. Hansen's quietly fierce way of grasping life and his pungent view of people were well worth the discipline I learned there—at seventeen.

Walter Watts was the pastor in Lake George. Now, all in all, if you are a pastor, Lake George is not going to put you on the map. There will be no Sunday morning services on national television, no book offers, and few speaking invitations other than a standing offer at Emmaville Town Hall. I might never have known Walt except that he had a darkroom in his basement. Thanks to my father introducing me to the community, I was offered a chance to use Walt's darkroom. Although I entered the darkroom as Earl's son, I emerged as Jim.

Walt taught me how to use his equipment and then said, "Replace the chemicals you use and you are free to use the darkroom whenever it is free." After the first few visits, I never worried about being welcome in Walt's house. Sometimes, after a long project, I would lock up the house as I quietly left Walt and his sleeping family. The skills I developed in Walt's darkroom provided me with several jobs over the years, but the trust of Walt and his family helped me become a responsible man and father. Walt was an elder who used his home, resources, and abilities to the benefit of his community.

Jim Schriber loved people. He was probably the sort of person anyone would think of as an elder. Jim kept bees and produced his own honey. I think his wife Jemimah baked bread; she served it too. He taught hundreds of boys to put honey on the bread first and butter second. "It keeps the honey in!" he would say. Hundreds of satisfied little boys agreed.

Jim collected tops. He had large tops, small tops, singing tops, upside-down tops. And he would do tricks with them. He spun tops on kids' heads, caught them in mid-air with their own strings, and almost never missed. Jim smiled, laughed, and talked to strangers as if he had always known them.

Jim loved to fish and take others fishing. Almost every day Jim had someone new with him in a boat full of people, teaching them to fish. His way was simple. He trolled up and down the lake with long bamboo poles for each guest until some northern pike would hit the lure. "Let's bamboozle them," he would always joke as he handed out the poles. All the while he talked, guided, taught about the lake, the fish, the birds, the weather, and how to enjoy the experience.

Back on shore, Jim taught his guests to fillet the fish, that is to say, they watched and he talked. In about thirty seconds per fish, supper was on its way. There was always bread, butter, and honey on the table.

One summer Jim taught me to fish, but he did more than that. He taught me how to care for the poles, maintain an outboard motor, balance a load of passengers in a boat, watch the weather, give people a safe ride, keep the lines from getting tangled, take fish off the hook, and help women and children feel comfortable fishing.

Jim was an elder, and I was a kid in the community. My dad and Jim worked at the same school. Because Jim cared about people, I had the best summer of my life. Jim found the people, bought gas for the boat, and I took them fishing. Sometimes I filleted the fish. It took about two minutes with no talking. And sometimes Jim made them fly into the pan in seconds amid cheers. Jim made me popular. He gave me a place and a skill, made me feel indispensable, all because he saw something in me.

Jim helped me find a place in a world of people and the world of nature. With each new boatload, he assured us all that I had something of value to give and we were all worth getting to know. To this day, I always have a little honey in the cupboard and put the butter on second to keep it in.

Last night we had Denver Rice for supper. Most folks have not tried Denver Rice because they haven't met Denver Brown. Denver's mother died when he young, and his wife died when he was old. Mentioning either one brings tears to his eyes, but what brings him to the door is that Denver keeps getting grandchildren. My children are Denver's grandchildren; he adopted them in his eighties. He loves to see how they are doing and remembers them on holidays.

Christmas morning he stopped by with Christmas lights

blinking all over his jacket to say, "Merry Christmas!" On his way he dropped off some special, high protein rice—Denver Rice. Before he left, he gave a blessing prayer and talked about the God who had brought him through the years.

Denver goes to the gym each day to work out and likes home-cooked meals. He wants nutritious food for his family. He filters his water and works five days a week. Denver has life to give and people to preserve and care for. Denver is an elder.

Earl is an elder in an unusual way. He is in his late seventies and loves the news. He listens to the news on TV and radio, as well as reading magazines and newsletters. Earl reads books on current issues and keeps informed. Earl is concerned for the nation and the world. Occasionally, when he sees someone on the news whom he admires, he writes to tell the person. When he hears something that concerns him, he writes to the individual and lets him or her know. He is always careful to show how he understands their position, so that they will not take him for a crackpot. Earl's concern is international, and many people experience his eldership unexpectedly in times of need.

Earl's home is open to community groups, foreign students, and resident aliens. He is on the local school board, teaches at the senior community center, and often teaches classes at church. He is learning his fourth language and grows his own vegetables in his garden. Earl appreciates life and gives it to others. His greatest concern is that everyone know of the life that comes only from God and through the life of Jesus come to spiritual life themselves. Earl is a life-giver. He is also my dad.

Willie is a teacher. Josie, his third wife, is a teacher. They have a daughter who works part-time in a school while attending college. Willie has the stuff to be a father. When his daughter grew up, he took in a relative from his wife's side of the family named Peter who was going to school near him. Willie could see that Peter was lost and needed a dad. Even though Peter proved to be self-centered and even a bit of a freeloader, Willie persevered. He had experienced enough losses to know the value of perseverance. There had been enough pain in his life to open his eyes. He saw that some people have to be loved just because a parent decides to love them. So it was that Willie loved Peter, talked to him, guided him, fed him, and housed him until Peter was ready to live on his own.

Dick is a young elder. It is only in the last year that he has learned the value of adoption. Dick knows something about giving. He was always willing to help others with their children, but drew back from adopting his own spiritual children even when his natural children had gone to college.

Dick grew up like a mighty oak in a forest of towering redwoods. His family included mighty men of faith, missionaries to China who would risk their lives for seven years to reach a town. Dick worked in advertising next to men with huge businesses and million-dollar projects, and famous writers with great ideas. The men in his life towered over him like mighty trees, so while to others he appeared a mighty oak, to himself Dick was a relatively small tree in a large forest.

Dick had a good heart. He and his wife Nancy found tires for people's cars and furniture for their homes, helped people save their homes from foreclosure, kept businesses from closing, helped folks promote their ideas, paid for treatment expenses of orphans, helped his church reduce its debt, brought words of encouragement and guidance to many people, and taught in church each week. But in spite of all these things Dick remained a small tree in his own mind.

As more and more of the great trees around him fell to the ground, Dick began to fear that the owner of the forest would seek his life as well, which indeed he did. God sought his life so that Dick might become a life-giver, not just a pain preventer. Dick had one of the worst years of his life. He had one trouble after another in a never-ending succession. Everything went wrong.

"The blessing is in the adoption we receive and give," Dick would teach. "Suffering and pain are part of the process." Teaching finally had its reward, for Dick found he needed to grow to match what he taught. Dick began to adopt little scruffy trees. Proof of his growth came when another friend lost his house. Dick said quietly to me, "I could not save him even if I had the money." For Dick now knew that the life he had to give did not consist of solving people's problems but in helping boys become men, men become fathers, and fathers become elders.

A NOTE OF CAUTION

Men need elders and this has always provided an opportunity for wolves to find sheep. The apostle Paul and others have pointed out that the hallmark of elders is their willingness to suffer for others without gaining power, control, money, or another advantage in return. Imposter elders are very sensitive to the needs of others and usually very warm in their concern, unless one crosses them or causes them any suffering, embarrassment, or loss of face. Young Americans flock to cults in great numbers seeking elders, with tragic results. An elder is one who believes it is more blessed for him to give and you to receive than the other way around.

It is hard to exaggerate the enrichment brought to their community by true elders. Men of all ages seek the secrets known by elders that will let them see themselves, the world, and God more clearly. Elders must seek out the younger men without fear, while the younger men look for the elders. In this way men will learn to be life-givers, not strangers.

Now we move on to the relationship of the elder with his daughters. After all, many women suffer from father hunger too.

FIFTEEN

The Elder and His Daughters

A S SHE GOT OFF THE BUS in Visalia, California, Arlis carried everything she owned in a handkerchief—not much for a fourteen-year-old girl. Mark Heinz was there to meet her. Even though she did not know him well, she recognized his smile. Mark and Gloria had sent the bus ticket that had brought her here. She tried not to think about her last time in this town.

Arlis' mother and her eight brothers and sisters moved a great deal. She had never stayed in one place long enough to complete even one semester in school. Visalia was one more town. Being naturally a little shy and retiring, Arlis had been glad when one of her classmates invited her home on Friday night.

"Can I spend the night?" she asked her mother.

Looking around the motel room the eight of them shared, her mother answered, "All right, but be back tomorrow morning to help me clean the room."

Saturday morning Arlis rode her bicycle back to the motel, but no one answered the door. Her mother had taken everything and everyone and left town—everyone but Arlis. Having no other idea of what to do, Arlis went back to the home she had visited overnight where they let her stay another day.

MARK AND ARLIS—FATHER AND DAUGHTER

Sunday morning she went to church. It was a small church, about forty people in all. Mark was the youth minister, Gloria was the director of music, and Mark's dad was the pastor. With their help, Arlis contacted her grandmother in Washington state who said she could come there to live. Before she left Mark took her aside. He was saddened by the loss this young girl faced. Wishing to set her mind at rest, he told her, "If you ever need a place to stay, we will help you find one."

Arlis got a ride to Washington with an associate pastor. She was about to take the bus the rest of the way to her grandmother's house, when Grandma abruptly changed her mind and told Arlis, "I don't want you here." Like that day in the motel, Arlis turned back to the place where she had just been to find help. She wrote to Mark.

"We knew it would impact our daughter Carol the most," Mark remembers, "so we asked her if she wanted an older sister. Carol had been an only child for eleven years, and we left the decision up to her." Suggesting that she pray about it for awhile, her parents waited two days for their answer. Carol now says that she could have given the answer at once, for she did want an older sister. So the bus ticket was sent and Arlis returned to Visalia.

Sitting in their living room that night, Mark told her, "You can't be a guest here. That just won't work. You will be part of the family." And as they talked, Arlis' confidence rose until she said, "Could I have a piece of bread?" The Heinzes realized suddenly that the girl had not had anything to eat, and Gloria hurried to the kitchen to fix her supper.

As they sat down to pray, Arlis asked if she could pray. It was a prayer that Mark never forgot. "Lord, help me to learn to obey my new mother and father," Arlis asked and with that request became a daughter to the only father she would ever really know.

"I made a commitment to Arlis then and there that she would be just like the daughter born to me," Mark remembers.

"It was instantaneous. The two girls became sisters and we were a family."

Arlis got her own room painted bright yellow, even though Gloria hated yellow. Arlis loved yellow. It was her room to do with as she wanted, and she kept her door tightly closed.

A few weeks later, Gloria, who was a bug about sleeping with fresh air, tiptoed into the girl's room to open a window. Arlis sat up screaming, clutching her blankets in terror. Mark and Gloria tried to comfort her to no avail. Hours later, the girl sobbed out, "If I tell you, then you won't like me any more."

"It won't change a thing," Mark told her. Taking courage from his words, the stories poured out. It seems she had been terribly abused and lived in terror of going to sleep at night. After the stories had been told, and the tears and the sobs had subsided, Arlis rested in the arms of those who would never allow such crimes to harm her again.

The door to Arlis' room was open after that, as was the door to her heart. "She loves me so much it's almost scary," Mark tells me almost forty years later. "It is the closest to the love I have with my heavenly Father that I have ever felt. Over the years we have continued to grow closer. I am a very blessed man.

"Some people think that it must be a sacrifice. We didn't have much money, but I am the one who was enriched. I only wish the church and my relatives could have accepted what our family accepted. They continued to refer to the girls as 'Arlis and your daughter' when they were both my daughters. My brother and sister have never really accepted my girl. They still invite us over and tell me not to bring Arlis. She still cries and is sad about that. Almost all her birth family has died and the family that should be hers won't have her."

Mark becomes tearful when he remembers how Arlis was blamed for Gloria's death because Arlis was divorced just as Gloria was dying. Some want to believe that the stress was the cause of Gloria's decline, but Mark does not believe it.

As a result of her divorce, Arlis was booted out of her church. Because of the divorce, the pastors at the church told Carol, Arlis' adoptive sister, that she should treat Arlis as though she were dead and never speak to her again. This drove a wedge between the two women which has never been removed. It brought contention between Carol and her father, who had always been extremely close. Arlis' children turned away from the church after seeing how their mother was treated.

"I just can't reconcile this rejection by my family and church with being a Christian," Mark told me sadly. "I can be Dad for my girl, but I can't be cousin, uncle, aunt, nephew, church, or sister." He nearly choked on the last word.

"If I could, I would ask them what the word forgiveness means. I would tell them of the joy and blessing they are missing. I have definitely gotten the best part of this bargain. They have really missed out."

Arlis was not the only girl that Mark and Gloria took into their home before Gloria died. The other girls were looking for a stand-in father but never adopted Mark, his family, his name, and his life the way Arlis did.

Having enjoyed being a practicing elder for forty years now, Mark still lights up like a Christmas tree at the mention of Arlis. Many times he has confided the same secret to me, always with the same pleasure and melody in his voice. His face breaks into a smile behind his white mustache. He leans forward ever so slightly and says, "She calls me, 'Dad,' and I call her 'daughter'!"

"Some people say that a thirty-year-old can't adopt a fifteen-year-old, but I did," Mark states with a certain tone of finality. In fact, the case with elders is that they often do what others say can't be done, or what others think should be done, but no one else will actually do. Elders see those who others view as strangers as family.

OTHER STORIES OF ELDERS AND WOMEN
IN THEIR CARE

Age is not a big hindrance to the way elders live. Glen has been around for three quarters of a century. In his younger days, he drove a delivery truck. Perhaps it was his wife's chronically disabled sister or his recovery from cancer that opened Glen's eyes to the needs around him, but he has never been so busy as he has since he retired. Besides volunteer work in the hospital, weekly visits to relatives in nursing homes, and care for his nieces, nephews, and grandchildren, Glen has become more than a friend to others in his mobile home park. When Sylvia had a stroke, Glen made sure that she got to the hospital, he looked after her trailer, managed her checkbook, and kept her life in order until Sylvia's daughter could be persuaded to take an interest. She is just one of many that Glen has seen through a time of crisis when they could not take care of themselves. It is very hard to be so sick that one is entirely at the mercy of others. As an elder, Glen took care of each one as he would have cared for his own child. Glen is a father to many widows and men in their old age.

Sam is an engineer and a craftsman. Sam designs and makes tiny parts for spacecraft. A decade or more after he should have retired, his company keeps him on as a master craftsman. Sam is not a talker, he quietly goes about his tasks. Every Saturday he takes two women from his neighborhood grocery shopping. They don't have cars and can't get around well. Perhaps it was Sam's wife's recurrent illness that helped him see the need in others. Whatever the source, he is there each Saturday. The women are very picky shoppers, partly due to their fixed incomes. Yet Sam patiently waits for them to finish shopping and then takes them home, where he helps fix the things that need care around their house without upsetting the two packrats that live there.

Francisco was a union foreman in a sugar processing plant. He had a small farm and raised a few farm animals. Francisco hated to see anything go to waste. As a result he rarely had an empty room in his small house. Mrs. Brown moved in after her husband's death. She had no money to speak of, and at eighty-five couldn't get a job, but she could make preserves. No fruit ever went to waste with Mrs. Brown around the neighborhood. She fed the chickens and helped Francisco's wife with the business she ran out of their house.

Mrs. Brown was not the only one to live in Francisco's house. His teenage niece roomed with his daughters after being neglected by her father. From time to time a missionary's son might stay awhile. Francisco knew the meaning of hospitality. He knew how to be a father to the men in his union and the women of his community.

Hospitality was also the hallmark of the Quail house. The Quails were parents to more college students than they could count. When the need arose to borrow a car, Dad Quail would turn over the keys, so a young man could get back to see his girlfriend. The Quails understood matters of the heart. In their home many nervous, insecure college students found a place to take a boy or a girl home and meet "Mom and Dad." Rare as it might seem to those who like to choose their dates and mates in bars, at poetry readings, cappuccino houses, or in video arcades, the Quails let their "adopted" children invite someone "home for dinner." Kids and their dates could come over for an evening, which included the comforts of home rather than the clutter of dorm rooms and the tackiness of Denny's Restaurant.

More than one woman who didn't know where or who her dad was found comfort in seeing Dad Quail talk to her date, even if she never talked directly to him about boys. To hear Dad Quail say, "You know that Bert is a fine young man," seemed to make a difference and reassured young women's hearts. He did what a father would do.

Last Easter Willard and Virginia Olwin had to sleep in their camper. They had seventeen house guests. Their granddaughters came down from San Francisco and invited three boys to visit them at Grandpa's house. The boys bicycled down for the weekend. It took them three days, but they had a great time. The granddaughters knew where to invite friends to visit. Still, that is not seventeen people. It turns out some visitors from Germany were in town, so with one thing or another, there were soon seventeen people happy to be "home" for Easter.

Willard is almost eighty and a retired salesman. He and Virginia travel regularly and encourage Christian leaders who at one time or another have enjoyed their hospitality. Willard is the precinct leader at the polls each election day. He looks after the grounds at church, is involved in several civic organizations and on the board of a camp, raises funds to send children to Christian summer sports clinic, serves meals each week at a homeless shelter, and collects and delivers food for needy families.

When I got out of graduate school and wanted to buy a house, Willard came to me one day and said, "If you need money for a down payment, I would be glad to lend it to you as I know your own parents are unable to do so." Being quite careful to protect my feelings, he expanded his offer to be a supplemental father to me and my family.

Wayne is only fifty-five, but he helps Willard in many ways. Some people in the community jokingly call Wayne "Willard Junior." It is more than a joke because Wayne has captured the spirit of fatherhood that Willard expresses. Both Wayne and Willard have adopted daughters from other countries and raised them. They have life to give and won't be stopped from giving it where it is needed. Neither one of them sees anything unusual about it.

Like Willard, Wayne also invested in me. Wayne put money in a business idea of mine that provided him, in the end, with a great tax write-off and gave me a taste of business failure. I crashed and burned but walked away to try again, thanks to elders like Wayne.

The interesting thing about elders is that they seem to find nothing unusual about what they do. They can't understand why everyone in their community doesn't join in and do likewise. Perhaps it is not that they don't understand, but rather that what is so compellingly natural to them is lacking in others. Elders can only wish it were not so. Elders see a need and find responding the only real alternative. While younger men often debate the rules, elders give the love because they have less room for fear.

These men have found it very rewarding to act as fathers to the women as well as the men in their communities. There is often more fear about men as fathers to women than men as fathers to other men. Perhaps this would be a good place to remember that elders have first been boys, then men, and then fathers before becoming elders. We are not talking about chronological years here. Being old guarantees nothing but wrinkly skin and more hair on your ears and other places where it does no good. True fathers and elders are very good for women, just as they are for men. They arrive there one stage at a time with no exceptions.

A famous woman writer who, in her seventies, is honored internationally by the Christian community told me that sometimes she really misses a father. She has had many fathers over the years, and they have now all died. She likes visiting with couples, but there are times when she yearns to go away alone with a father and pour out her heart to his undivided attention and hear what a father would say to his girl. We are never too old to have a good father.

A NOTE OF CAUTION

Women who, like men, need fathers and elders are also open to exploitation by wolves. This exploitation is usually financial, but can often be sexual as well. While any kind of relationship between men and women is viewed with suspicion and even alarm these days, elders can be distinguished in due time by their desire to live openly in their community and have their fathering examined, improved upon, and emulated by others. Wolves do not desire this review, although at times they brag shamelessly about themselves to their followers.

It is also well known that many Christian leaders who have affairs start out feeling fatherly towards the woman. This affection later turns to lust and disaster. In every such case I have examined, the man has reached elder status prematurely having skipped stages, passages, and, above all, having failed to learn what really satisfies his need for intimacy. Having unlocked a need he did not know he had, he sought to fulfill a need he did not know how to satisfy. Instead of turning to an elder who would teach him what really satisfies, he turned to a woman and solitary prayers of desperation. Any man or woman stuck in or fleeing such a situation should know that what they originally desired was good and turn to elders who will help them find true satisfaction. You will not find it alone.

Our churches and society could benefit from some good teaching about elders and their daughters. Since few people seem to understand this important role, some women become prey to wolves while others, like Arlis, never find acceptance. Perhaps when we know how to think about elders and their relationships, we will be able to support and participate in the joy Mark describes, "She calls me 'Dad,' and I call her 'daughter'!"

Now that we have explored an elder's relationships with his sons and daughters, we need to ask what sort of an impact the elder can make on the life of the church—our family—as an important source of our life and the keeper of our redemptive history?

SIXTEEN

Elders and the Church

S OME DREAMY, HOT SUMMER AFTERNOON, as clouds drift through deep blue skies over the tops of houses and trees, stop a moment. With a cool glass of lemonade in your hand, watch the leaves rustle and stop a moment. Everything you see is real, but there is something more. Beyond that blue sky are stars, lights without number; even though you can't see them now, they are there. Constellations and galaxies just beyond your sight wait for dark, so you may know their beauty. Beyond the stars, beyond the night, there is even more you cannot see quite yet. The Father of Lights lives there. His presence passes down through the stars which we see only momentarily to the world under the blue sky, the world of lemonade people.

Here, beneath a thousand shade trees, are his people, the sons and daughters of the resurrection, the bride of the Eternal One. Together, one and all love each other with a deep eternal love in the unity of joy. All are one family—*The Family*. Boys and girls, men and women, fathers and mothers, and elders live right here next to you in the family of God. Can you see it, or does *The Family* hide from your eyes like the stars in the afternoon sky?

It is in the context of *The Family* that the stages and passages of life are best lived out. The community provides a continuity of life and the wealth of resources needed to help each individual grow, each family form, and each generation build on the last. Elders hold a special claim to this community life. They are the guardians of *The Family*.

If we consider the church to be a family, the support of enduring, eternal relationships with parents, children, brothers, and sisters of faith is made possible by God. It is he who provides the fruits of the Spirit evident in every believer. And whether they have found their gifts yet or not, all God's children belong in this family.

The church is a family. The elders are parents in this family and provide enduring relationships. This is obviously a central role to which all mature believers may well aspire. *The Family* exists for each other so that there will always be enough goodness to go around and some to spare. Elders dispense this goodness to their children. First Thessalonians 5:14 instructs elders to "warn those who are idle, encourage the timid, help the weak, be patient with everyone." The church of God is supposed to be about precisely such things.

While the church contains a full range of family members, many church groups appear to an outside observer to be homogenous units that are more interested in preservation of resources than in having "children." There is often the appearance of stratification within *The Family* by age and resources. Sometimes the stratification is between congregations. A city may contain two churches, one full of the poor and the other full of the rich, one full of the youth, another full of the aged. In larger churches, Sunday school classes and social groupings are fixed by age and wealth, the presence of children, married or single status, ethnic or racial heritage, and whether one is an old-timer or a stranger. Even within the church strangers tend to be grouped with strangers, widows with widows, orphans with orphans. These bonds between strangers are easily broken if a struggle for resources ensues. Struggles for resources are common in stratified church families.

It should not be imagined that the resources I am talking about are primarily financial. Time, love, care, comfort, company, attention, encouragement, and belonging are often needed far more than cold cash. We all need *The Family*. We all need adoption.

In Bangladesh, I am told, when a person accepts Christ, that person is immediately ostracized by his or her biological and social family. The Christian church then provides a family that adopts the new convert as its own. Family growth is viewed as a good thing. As David pointed out, the line of the ungodly is cut off (loses a member), but the line of the righteous endures (gains a member) (Ps 109; Ps 127).

The purpose of all church life should include the edification of the body with the clear expectation that, just as we raise children to have children of their own, so it is in the church family. Elders, fathers, and mothers teach ministry by example in the hope that others will also grow and minister. It is not for the purpose of training others that they minister. To make training the sole purpose of ministry insults God and the recipient. We do not care for our children simply so that they will grow up to have children. Some will never grow up and others will never have children. But our lives should enhance their desire and ability to live as we have lived. In this way the family is carried on and grows, whether it is human or spiritual.

Perhaps the greatest enemy of elders in America is not our disrespect for the old, the rapid change of society, or the obsolescence of knowledge, but greed. An elder is not to be greedy, according to the apostle Paul, and indeed cannot be effective if his desires run towards his own comfort. Greed, envy, and jealousy are mentioned by the apostle James as the source of trouble in *The Family*. Greed is seen most often in the form of "wealth preservation," that is, holding on to what we have.

It is understood in America that having too many children will lead to excessive loss of wealth. Children and family are a liability to those who wish to reduce expenses and preserve wealth. Young adults wait to have children until they can afford them—all the while buying fancy cars, ski lift tickets, well-heeled educations, and videocassette recorders. Older people even have bumper stickers that read, "We are spending our children's inheritance." All of these forms of greed agree that money is best spent on *me*. This thought can be beautiful as a sentiment in a child, but it is always ugly in an adult. Greed is the hallmark of the dissatisfied person, more proof that childhood goals were never reached among greedy people. Having never completed the childhood tasks means that the greedy individual is not close to being ready for the demands of manhood, let alone status as an elder.

Wealth preservation is a form of greed frequently found in churches, and in people of all ages. Keeping a standard of living and holding on to what they earn is a major focus for many people. Some don't want to lend things to people who will not return them or might wreck them, even in the face of clear instructions from Jesus that we should lend to those who can't repay. The same is true for lending money. Some will only lend to those who pose no risk of loss. Others carefully include only the people who will provide their own resources and exclude those who will deplete their supplies. Whether it is choosing whom to invite out for dinner or who will share a vacation, considerations usually favor those who will pay their own way.

The notion of having a large family or having more children seems expensive to many Americans. Consequently, having more children seems more like a curse than a blessing. Yet God has decreed that one blessing due his faithful followers is to have many descendants. Elders seek this blessing. Elders work to see their family grow and invest accordingly. Elders cannot have too many children or seek to keep all their wealth for themselves and their "real" children.

The Scripture makes over one hundred references to the "stranger." The stranger is one who lacks the *necessary* supportive relationships and can, therefore, be easily ignored or used by others. Strangers are mentioned in the company of widows and orphans, who obviously suffer from the same set of problems. The treatment of these groups becomes the test of true religion for the Old Testament prophets. According to Christ, it is also the final test when the sheep and goats are separated before the

Great White Throne. Supporting the unsupported is the church's business.

It would seem that with so much attention given in Scripture to the care of others, greed would be almost unheard of in *The Family.* Such is not the case. This greatly concerns many family members who, over the years, have tried to correct the situation. To many it has been obvious that greed is a childish reaction. Children never seem to say, "That is enough," just as greedy people never quit trying to acquire more for themselves. Conventional wisdom has focused on raising children differently so as to prevent greed. Much effort has been spent and misspent exactly at this point.

Children who are taught to meet their own needs well are ready to understand the needs of others as equal to their own when they become adults. From there it is possible to move to sacrificial giving as modeled by fathers, mothers, and elders. Greed is fed by the secret gnawing dissatisfaction of those who live in fear and guilt over their own needs. Many strive to place their "self" on the altar before they are fully grown. They are like a boy whose father planted a grove of trees.

"Son," he said, "one day when you are grown and your children are grown these trees will provide fine wood like those trees on the hill." He pointed to a grove of stately giants. The boy was impressed.

One day the son noticed a group of men working in the grove of mature trees. It was hot and the men labored hard cutting down the trees. This strenuous labor went on for weeks until at last all the wood had been harvested. A few days later the father went out to his little grove. To his dismay he found every last sapling neatly cut off at the ground with his boy standing, quite satisfied, in the middle of them all.

"What have you done my son!" cried the father.

"Oh, Father! I have just spared my children much suffering," came the reply. "When I saw how hard those men had to work cutting down the trees, I realized how much time and effort would be spared by cutting these trees now. Why, I have done in one hour what took many men weeks to do!"

Sacrificial giving before there is a solid self is like cutting down a baby tree. The result is little wood and little lasting satisfaction. This is the breeding ground for greed, the fear of never having enough, of guilt for having anything, and the mortal enemy of the elder and community. Greed is a deadly enemy to children and their need for authentic blessing.

Each stage of growth must be built on a solid foundation or the next stage becomes a mockery of manhood. Each passage must result in a new identity or we become caterpillars with glued-on wings rather then butterflies. Guilt-motivated giving is not love and masks the value and joy in suffering for others which is genuine to elders. We must begin with the truth about ourselves.

It seems to me that most of us still have some growing up to do, but let's be honest. Those who haven't finished being boys yet need to start by being boys. Those who are waiting to make the passage to manhood must start there. It is foolish to try to skip a step just because you have been on the planet longer than your development would indicate. Remember that no passage in a man's life can successfully be made alone. Birth needs Mother, weaning needs Father, manhood needs other men, fatherhood needs the family, elders need the community, and the dying need God.

Every passage in our lives is made successfully through much hard work. Yet the work is not all our own, but also that of those who went this way before. Our family is around us now— if only we could see them. So let us leave behind our isolation and seek the eyes of heaven that we may best see our history and the true faces of our family.

THE CHURCH AS OUR SOURCE OF LIFE

Where else can we find our sense of family and history than among our brothers and sisters in Christ, and among our spiritual fathers and mothers? I'm referring, of course, to the church as the source of life for God's people. Churches should be places where children learn of God's pleasure in meeting their needs. When the prophet Samuel was a little boy and lived in the temple, he enjoyed feasts in the house of God. They were provided by the priests who were like fathers to him and others who served there. He knew that God would provide for him. In fact, after the sacrifices, there was always enough food for the priests and their assistants, as well as some left over for the people.

Under the direction of the elders, what better place is there than the church—*The Family*—to take boys through their rite of passage into manhood? Is there any other tradition of redemptive history to which we may turn? After all, the church radically redefines our sense of family and community, even our sense of being part of a nation or country. It gives us a long lineage of prophets, patriarchs, matriarchs, kings, queens, priests, apostles, and saints as a basis for our life. Our line even includes the Son of God himself.

It is in this community that men and women should find their stories told and retold, reminding them why they are alive. It is in *The Family* that boys and girls should begin to learn why they are alive, under the tutelage of the elders.

Men will, if left to be shaped by the demands placed on them, become life-receivers or life-givers, but rarely both givers and receivers. To do one without the other renders a man unbalanced and ineffective. In the church, we have the opportunity to hear both sides of the story repeated each week. For it is precisely here that we receive our bodies and our lives from God, and then go out to give them away to others.

Tragically, elders who want more children and have this wonderful life to give away tend to be the missing part of American church life, as far as I can tell. Who can say what would happen if there were a group of elder men in each church eager for larger families—elders who were waiting, able, and happy to raise more children?

It is good to be male when that is what we are. It is good to receive life and then to give it again. It is good to pass from glory to glory. It is good to be on the journey home with *The Family* close by our side.

That journey home leads us to death—the last passage in an elder's life. Witnessing an elder's death can be one of the most meaningful experiences in life among members of *The Family*.

SEVENTEEN

The Death of an Elder

"I never knew dying was such hard work." Walter Gilbert

I T WAS HIS WORK THAT FINALLY KILLED HIM. Like many men, Walter worked hard. Teaching chemistry was rewarding for him, but in the end it might well have been the prolonged exposure to chemicals that produced the emphysema which led to his death. During his last days on earth, Wayne visited Walter. In the course of their conversation, Walter noted with surprise how hard it was to die. A few days later he died surrounded by friends and loved ones. His work was over.

Death is the last passage we are able to observe in a man's life, and then only from this side of eternity. Like all passages, death leads to a new identity, one we can't really understand ahead of time. Yet, for those who passed through weaning, from being boys to being men, from men to fathers, and from fathers to elders, there develops a certainty that such passages are not only possible but highly desirable. Elders know that we can survive the unknown and unknowable. They have already survived at least four transformations and have learned the art of expectancy. Those who have watched elders die have noticed this keen expectancy. It is something that Christians call hope.

For our own good, and in order to know this expectancy, we should never let an elder die alone. Their last great gift to us is the expectancy of safe passage and transformation. This hope is a blessing to people of all ages and stages.

We do not need to fear the death of an elder. Unweaned children, when accompanied by good parents, can draw courage from an elder's expectancy for their upcoming weaning. Boys can face the unknown changes in their bodies and the weighty implications of their histories through sharing this expectancy. Men can give their lives away to their children knowing that in the end all will be purified by death. Elders can give freely to others with the certainty that soon they, too, will take with them only the life they have given away and leave behind all that they have kept.

While it is good for males of all ages to gather when an elder dies, the same is not true of the deaths of the unprepared. Those who cannot face death are a great trauma to be near in their final moments. In such cases, fathers and elders should stay close, while children should clearly be kept away. Like all transformations, success is not automatic and the process is not inevitably good.

At times, some youngsters with a terminal disease will be given a readiness for metamorphosis which is beyond their years. Perhaps it is the experience of surviving the negative transformations of disease that allows these young travelers their peaceful expectancy. But it is also the certainty expressed by their elders that such change is possible which quiets their souls.

Like all passages, death is accomplished by each person alone and yet to succeed requires the help of others. Each elder must uniquely experience his own transformation, but without help this transformation will end in disaster, for none can give birth to themselves or see themselves through death.

Death itself represents the final decontamination of man from all that is not life-giving. Precisely for this reason it is dangerous, for should the man prove not to be life-giving, he will find this last visible passage leading to permanent death rather than permanent life. Like all parts of his history, he will not be able to undo the consequences of his actions on those who will then follow him.

Death builds on the stages that have gone before. Those who have received and given life go on to permanent life, while those who have refused to receive or give life go on to permanent death. Precisely because of the seriousness of this passage, there is a tendency towards deathbed conversions. For those who care to leave a legacy of hope and life to their loved ones, this last act is life-giving and will serve to see them through decontamination, for they have received and given life. Others seeking to beat God's judgment on their lives make such last-minute conversions to try and cancel their bad record. In so doing they make a mockery of Jesus' death, as if to say, "Better him than me." Thus their last act is death-giving. Having neither received or given life, they will die permanently. This attempt to cheat God of his justice is what the church has called the mortal sin of *presumption*.

Although we all must die, we do not consider all deaths alike. We sense an inner revulsion to anyone who tries to take the passage to death out of turn. That is why suicide is so awful. We bear a special grief when babies and children die too. Mourners keep saying, "It is such a pity," and similar expressions of exceptional grief in such situations. When teenagers die, we have a similar response. Yet because we know more of their history, we have more to remember with the loss of such a young life. How many of us can remember being teens and saying, at least to ourselves, "I don't want to die before I fall in love, get married, make love, or have children." Such are the dreams of youth.

So too, the death of a father is a tragedy to his family. "What will his wife and children do now?" we wonder. Although the sense of loss for the man himself is far less than it would be for a teenager or child, we mourn the loss of the life he would yet have given. There is less of a sense that he died before he had a chance to live. And yet fathers have their dreams as well. I can clearly remember my father telling me that because he married late and had his first son at thirty-eight, he feared he would not live to see his grandchildren. I remember my satisfaction at presenting his first grandchild to him and my deep secret joy that he was wrong.

Considering how little we like seeing death taken out of turn, one would think that the entire community would devote itself to helping every member achieve each stage of growth and successfully negotiate each passage into the next stage. It is elders who direct and best understand such concerns. This is one reason why many family members fear the loss of their influence. As elders approach death, their families wait for blessing and direction from them. It is impossible for younger people to completely imagine themselves filling the elder's shoes. They do not know what elders know. Often it is clear that the next generation has less character and resolve than their elders. They need blessing and instruction before the elder leaves.

THE BLESSING

The time around the death of an elder has always been connected with great blessing. Jacob blessed his children on his deathbed. Elijah blessed Elisha, who received a double portion of the spirit and power his mentor experienced, when he stayed close enough to see the fiery chariot take his teacher away.

Sadly no one sought the spirit from Elisha when he died, so his blessing stayed with him. True, King Jehoash came for a blessing, calling him, "My father, my father!... The chariots and horsemen of Israel!" (2 Kgs 13:14). But the king was only thinking of the military protection he was losing, not the blessing he might receive, so all he got was three victories in battle. Years later, when some men were hurriedly burying a dead man, they tossed him in the prophet's grave when they caught sight of enemy raiders approaching. The blessing that was still with the prophet caused the man to come back to life and stand up when his body touched Elisha's bones (2 Kgs 13:20-21).

There is something about a man who has walked with God for many years that is very special. Perhaps it is the simplicity he has developed. When Dirk Zweibel retired from psychology, he told his younger colleagues, "I have learned that theoretical models, techniques, and practice do not replace love. Love is what matters."

A few years ago my father, who was then in his early seventies, told me, "I have learned to say little about the matters where Scripture is not clear and hold strongly where it bears no equivocation."

Merv Dirks, whose very presence brings a sense of well-being to a room, recalled to me that his dad was a man who walked with God. "I always wanted to emulate him. For my dad it wasn't a complicated thing. He had a really simple walk with God. It was like a little child walking with his father. That is not complicated or profound!" Then Merv laughed. He told me we should love each other. No one is around him for very long before they know that to Merv it is that simple.

With all of the wisdom, love, patience, and grace which elders possess there come the penalties of older age. Elders see many opportunities which they lack the energy to pursue. That is why elders really need fathers, young men, and boys to surround them. What the elder sees but cannot accomplish himself can become an excellent training ground for younger men in the context of real encouragement.

Elders also complain of loneliness. Particularly difficult is the lack of appreciation by others for those things that really matter. Elders look at the world differently and really need each other in order to talk with someone who understands without having to question their point of view. It is like the difference between explaining a joke and having someone "get it." Elders like to talk and pray with other people who do "get it."

One Saturday, the day before Easter, Gary Bayer and I were walking around a monastery for our usual morning prayer time when we were greeted by a very old man who was walking energetically up the hill. He smiled and stopped to talk. There was something warm, unguarded, and open in his manner. His white hair, what little there was of it, was tied behind his head in a little ponytail.

"Do either you espeak Espanish?" he asked. "*Vengan a comulgar,*" he said, opening his mouth and putting in imaginary food, then tossing back his head as he downed an imaginary cup. He gestured with such vigor and zest that Gary and I had to laugh.

"Come, come *a comulgar*. It is Holy Saturday. God love you! I love you! Come!" He hugged us with delight.

"Come, my sons!" he said again and repeated the gestures with the bread and the cup. "I will pray for you!" With that he hugged us again with such spontaneous joy that Gary and I giggled like two schoolgirls. This elder had no fear, no embarrassment, no hesitation about what life meant.

"I want to be like him," Gary told me as we reached the car. At once I sensed how far I still had to travel down the road to love.

"I wonder if we met an angel," I said. It somehow didn't seem possible that a man could exude such love and have such a lack of fear.

"We were blessed this morning," Gary said.

These are the blessings from the elders—the lack of fear with which they face life and death, the freedom with which they love, and their simple certainty of how they want to live. This is the way they see others, their understanding of death and resurrection, the expectancy they bring to Holy Saturday.

Jesus' death was also a time of great blessing. He had a special feast and blessed his disciples on the night before he was betrayed and then faced death. Even on the cross, those who stood close to him received blessings. The centurion saw who Jesus really was; Mary received a son; John, a mother; and we received the safe passage we needed through death. Now that one in human form has passed that way successfully, all those who follow him may likewise receive the initiation of his death into new life.

All our passages prepare us for death. And the death of an elder, when properly observed, prepares us for the lesser transformations we face in this life. Stay close to an elder in *The Family* and watch that last step! It will change the way you view your life forever.

Notes

SEVEN
How Sons Become Men

1. This was formerly entitled *Just Between Father and Son: How a Weekend Trip Prepares a Boy for Adolescence* and published by InterVarsity Press. It is now out of print. As *Rite of Passage: How to Teach Your Son about Sex and Manhood*, it is scheduled to be published by Servant Publications in the summer of 1994.

TEN
Fathers and Their Children

1. Octavio Paz, *The Labyrinth of Solitude* (New York: Grove Press, 1961), 82.
2. Paz, *The Labyrinth*, 82.
3. Paz, *The Labyrinth*, 82.
4. John Fischer, "Christopher's Toes" (Waco, Texas: Word Music, 1982), ASCAP.

THIRTEEN
Becoming an Elder

1. In many Christian and pseudo-Christian traditions, *elder* refers to a particular church office. Most Protestant denominations use *elder* to

refer to a church board member. These individuals are usually elected to run the church or oversee operations. The Nazarene Church uses *elder* to refer to its ordained clergy. The Latter Day Saints (Mormons) also employ the term for their missionaries and leaders. Scripture also contains descriptions of *elders* in 1 Timothy and Titus. Timothy, it appears, was not himself an elder and, although he was a church leader, is instructed to correct *elders* as he would a father.

2. Wayne Watson, "Somewhere in the World" (Waco, Texas: Word Music, 1985), ASCAP.

Another Book by the Author That Will Interest Vine Book Readers

Rite of Passage
How to Teach Your Son about Sex and Manhood

E. James Wilder

Here is a book for parents that will help them prepare their sons for the exciting, puzzling, and sometimes frightening journey from boyhood into manhood. *Rite of Passage* will also be of interest to churches with men's groups. It is designed so that Dad can take a weekend trip with his pre-adolescent son as a rite of passage into manhood, just as Wilder recounts in these pages his own weekend adventure with his then twelve-year-old son Jamie.

Whether Dad makes it a weekend, or a single mom or men's group uses the material in some other context, Dr. Wilder provides frank, positive, and faith-filled advice on helping boys on the verge of puberty cope with the pressures of sex, drugs, self-esteem, peer groups, and more. Every Christian family with sons and every church active in the men's movement will find *Rite of Passage* an invaluable resource. Scheduled for release in the summer of 1994.

$8.99